Rhyme & Reason

Published by DPK Publishing—AscensionForYou

Paperback ISBN: 978-1-914936-15-9
e- ISBN: 978-1-914936-16-6
Hardcover ISBN: 978-1-914936-24-1

Rhyme & Reason

Copyright ©2021 by David P. Knight

Formatted by E. Rachael Hardcastle of Curious Cat Books

All rights reserved and the moral right of the Channeller/Author has been asserted. Without limiting the rights under copyright reserved above, no part of this publication may be reproduced, stored in or introduced into a retrieval system, or transmitted, in any form, or by any means (electronic, mechanical, photocopying, recording, or otherwise) without the prior written permission of both the copyright owner and the above publisher of this book.

A CIP catalog record for this book is available from the British library.

www.AscensionForYou.com

Rhyme & Reason

Spiritual Poetry and Prose to
Strengthen Your Heart, Uplift Your Soul, and
Define Your Purpose

By David Knight

Also by David Knight

Pathway

Deliverance of Love, Light and Truth

I Am I: The Indweller of Your Heart—Book One

I Am I: The Indweller of Your Heart—Book Two

I Am I: The Indweller of Your Heart—Book Three

I Am I: The Indweller of Your Heart— Collection

Leave the Body Behind—Sojourns of the Soul

A Pocket Full of God

If you enjoyed reading *Rhyme & Reason*, you can download *Deliverance of Love, Light, and Truth* for free when you join David's mission for a 'full and blissful life'.

Visit: AscensionForYou.com

"To know we all are 'one', part of the creator—GOD, the source, the Great White Spirit ... is such a wonderful and beautiful thing". **DK**

PREFACE

God is everywhere—omnipotent—but how often do we stop what we are doing to feel his/her presence? God loves us, but how many times in our lives have we forgotten the power of healing and the mercy and grace, and protection given upon our minds and bodies and souls? And God always speaks to us, so why don't we take time out of our day to listen to the guidance that he/she shares?

Perhaps you do … or maybe you can't. Yet for me, it's now over 25 years since I hoped and prayed that 'spirit' would communicate with, and through, me. I needed to understand more about our human existence. I wanted to know about our purpose here on the Earth. And was there really life after death? And who might guide me, so that I may also help others find their own truth too? There were so many questions … and I wanted the answers.

I was impatient and started attending spiritual development circles and meditation groups, which soon helped me to focus beyond the boundaries of my senses. Every sojourn (soul journey), within this physical realm, allows us to experience, which brings knowledge and wisdom to the body, mind, and soul. Karma plays its part too, as does our genetic memory and make up.

These, along with many precognitive dreams and journeys upon the ethereal planes and dimensions of God's kingdom and creation, taught me to listen … but not by hearing. And I soon realised this was another way for us to grow as human beings.

One day, a voice spoke through my mind. I didn't hear the words but felt them inside me … 'clear hearing' or clairaudience, some say. Over the weeks, months, and years, spirit guides came and went. Entities and beings from other planes, and Angels and archangels, and even Jesus blessed me with their presence … to share their love for the world and remind me of our own divine spark. During such times, their grace and beautiful 'light' brought forth many tears from the well of truth inside me.

One day, something changed. It was subtle at first, but the resonance and feeling when 'words' flowed appeared to materialise in what I can only describe as a direct connection to God. Some people also describe God as 'source', while others state that this only implies a to and from, as if it defines limitation … but names are irrelevant.

Know that love is unlimited, and the human mind cannot truly comprehend the reality of the 'creator' … the divine. And so, it began. I listened to my inner voice … my speaking heart and had my own conversations with 'God'.'

Please understand that this collection of poems arises from moments of stillness. Only in the silence can you expect to receive what you need to know and understand. Terms such as channelling or automatic writing are meaningless.

Ultimately, we are each given what we need in life … and when. Therefore, do not concern yourself about how important or unimportant you think you are, because every grain of sand is vital, for it makes us whole.

So, I hope you will allow Rhyme & Reason to calm an inflamed mind. May it also soothe a troubled or broken heart … and uplift your soul to reveal your true potential and destiny of joy and peace and eternal bliss. Or perhaps, just one poem can be the spark you need to reignite the flame of your true desire, to allow the fragrance of your divine petals to bloom and radiate the perfume of love into eternity. God bless and good luck on your continued journey. (Dave—AFY).

ACKNOWLEDGMENTS

Dear God, words cannot describe the peace and love you have sent to me. Without you, this work and book would never have been completed!

A SPECIAL 'THANK YOU'

To my wife Caroline for all her love, support, and encouragement ... and for all those upon the different planes and dimensions of creation who connect through my speaking heart.

TABLE OF CONTENTS

PREFACE	7
ACKNOWLEDGMENTS	9
A SPECIAL 'THANK YOU'	10
SEARCH FOR YOUR PATHWAY	15
THE MYSTERY	16
SO YOU SOW, SO SHALL YOU REAP	17
THE TEACHER	18
I SHALL ALWAYS BE	20
A PLEA	21
AN OPEN DOOR	22
ENTER	23
THE SPARK	24
LOVE AND LIGHT FROM THE GREAT SPIRIT ABOVE!	25
FLOW	26
INTENSITY	28
TREE OF LIFE	29
EMOTIONS	30
CURRENCY	31
COMPASSION	32
THE GAME	33
WHAT IS LOVE?	34
THE POWER OF LOVE	36
DECISIONS	38
TRUST	39
ENERGY AND FLOW	41
DANNY	42
A NEW ERA	43
WONDER	44
REACH OUT	45
AN ENLIGHTENED EXPERIENCE	46
THE WELL	47

THE SHELL	48
SERVICE	49
HEAVEN AND THE PLANES	50
RESISTANCE	51
SOMETHING NEW	53
MOVING ON … BE 'ONE'	54
HEAVEN'S DOOR	55
REGRESSION	56
A FRIEND'S MESSAGE	57
TO OPEN … AND EXPLORE	59
ARCHANGEL MICHAEL	60
NO DIVISION	61
KNOWN AND FOUND	62
THE TUNNEL	63
BEYOND	64
EXPLORE	66
MOMENTUM	67
ANGUISH	69
SHHH…	70
CHOICE	71
ETERNITY	73
REFLECTION	74
RECONNECTION	75
LIGHT AND SIGHT TO NEW LEVELS	76
YOUR SECRET TREASURE	78
A CHRISTMAS CAROL	79
STAR OF WONDER	80
KEEP ON TRACK … WITH SAI BABA	83
A SOUL'S GOAL	85
TRUTH	86
ENLIGHTENMENT	87
CONNECTIONS	92
EVERYTHING … I AM	94
1000 ('I's)	96
REUNION	97
I AM	99
I ACCEPT	100

RECOGNITION	101
OUR TEARS	102
REFLECTIONS	104
DEAR FATHER	105
DISCOVERY	106
STARS	107
THE PEARL	108
THE STRUGGLE	109
TIME	110
IF	111
SPIRIT AND SOUL	112
ISSY'S THANK YOU	113
FURTHER READING	114
GLOSSARY	117
ABOUT THE AUTHOR	132
AN INVITATION FROM DAVID KNIGHT	133

SEARCH FOR YOUR PATHWAY

I woke so confused in the beginning that was true,
Surely there is more to life than feeling so down and so "blue".
I asked, "Where do I look and what shall I find?"
Then a voice replied, "Just open your heart, your soul and your mind".

So, I turned 'within' and found truth, guidance, and love,
It came from the eternal spirit, the divine, the Almighty above.
With a light so beautiful, it shone all around,
And you will see too, it's not so hard to be found.

Follow this forever, because you will never be lonely, cold, or lost,
As on your 'pathway' you will discover, it doesn't even cost.
Have courage, conviction and sharing faith, it is a plus,
Each day at a time, no need to run or to rush.

On your journey meeting people and good friends they will become,
You'll get 'there' I do promise, 'til your PATHWAY is then done.
So be kind and also true, to yourself and fellow 'man',
Give it a try ... as deep inside, you (and I) both know that you can.

THE MYSTERY

In my dream herein a beauty lies,
Is it clear this meaning or is something disguised?
A race seems on within my mind and I,
Try as I might, to unravel these words 'inside'.

In my heart of mine, please, please I yearn so much,
For knowledge, wisdom, truth, and guidance and for love.
Forgive me Father for I felt lost and bewildered, but know I have found,
That you're always with me, your 'light' teaching me, and I won't let you down.

SO YOU SOW, SO SHALL YOU REAP

Light expands Light,
Love expands Love,
Desire expands the fire.

The flame expands God's name,
The name expands the 'grain',
The 'grain' expands the same,
The same holds no blame.
Now blame can hold distain,
And disdain retains the shame,
For shame can lead to blame.

The circles round again,
And 'one' you shall remain.
Until light has led the way,
It's eternal and a day.

(Then now realise)

A shining Star is both far and near,
So, search within and do not fear.
It radiates with love and light,
And our hearts are entwined all day and night.

Know that rose-coloured glasses or a blurred vision,
Can erase or fade your soul's true mission.
That you and 'all' exist to grow,
To ascend the cord that you will sow.

THE TEACHER

Do not worry or concern yourselves where each of you come from, for no matter how different you all appear to be, you are the same, yes, all the same to your 'Father' and to me. Precious, like flowers and the drops of the rain … which bring sustenance and nourishment and never in vain. You'll glow and radiate and spiral around, for love, true love, it knows no bounds.

You'll also reach out and search both far and wide, overseas and the land and you'll look to the sky. Sometimes there'll be pain and sometimes there'll be joy and the gift of a new-born child is indeed not a toy. With a chance to fulfil and to also instil, find the love from above, taking flight like a dove.

Angels and Archangels in Heaven and on Earth both look and assist the meek and the mirth. Some are below and some are above, all with their 'work' from the Lord and our God. To aid and assist you in all that you do, be glad, be safe, for He and I are in you. Go north, south, east, and west, just try to do all, with love and your best. And so…

Different rooms of the house, but hearts are all safe,
For God has enveloped and surrounded you with a 'fate'.
For you are all 'from' and return unto Him,
So, rejoice and all sing just like love within a hymn.

You will all grow, as I have just said,
Just try to believe and rise up from your bed.
Whether morning or noon or evening or night,
The days that you walk will remain always bright.

The golden 'Son' forever glows, deep within your hearts,
Can never be extinguished or be divided into parts.
For each segment, each band, and vibration or sound,
Is eternal and, as stated, true love knows no bounds.

Rhyme & Reason

Each day is a link, and the chain keeps you all,
No 'separation and division', or an 'unearthly' fall.
So even if your life then hits a new low,
Call unto your 'Father', for he already knows.

Of what you require and of what you would all like,
To happen and 'emerge', yes from 'within' and out life.
Just 'be' and to ask with all of your heart,
For the Lord knows too, of what's right from the start.

The teacher is no man or with a false text,
It is the light and the love that is 'within' that's the test.
So, justify the why and then hear the call,
To know then dear 'children', you can never, ever fall.

Just be 'still'; be still … for you are the 'divine',
And you are all 'one'… and each are all mine.
Not a possession cast aside or washed up by the tide,
For the crown of my heart, I give freely, openly, and I will never, ever hide.

I SHALL ALWAYS BE...

The boat, which carries you across the ocean(s) of your emotions.
The land you walk upon holding you upright and true.
The wind, to blow dark clouds away from your body, mind, and soul.
The spiritual 'vision' to reveal the light ... and the Sun to radiate warmth and love in your heart.
The hand that lifts you up from the ground when you feel you cannot go on.
The life giving 'water', to quench your thirst for truth, knowledge, and wisdom.
The spark deep within you, which gives you everlasting life.
The colours of the rainbow, shining down upon your darkened days of false fears and tears.

We are '**one**' forever, so please do not grieve. Erase the heartache and pain, as you are eternal joy ... now live, breathe, know, and understand this. Appreciate love conquers all things that you could ever possibly imagine fearing ... so do not, as you are nearer than near to me. I love you all. Amen.

A PLEA

Love is a wondrous thing ... to be shared by every <u>living</u> thing,
So do not judge each other, but be kind to one another.
It is simple this message from the heart,
That we are all one, right from the start.

My heart does 'bleed' ... for you not to kill each other so,
It is not for me to judge you though,
But just remember this,
How much love do you give ... in a 'loving' kiss?

AN OPEN DOOR

The doorway is right here, so it is time to turn the key,
But what will you then find, and is it just for me?
Well, open the door, just a fraction maybe more,
And take a peep inside, for love and the light it does not hide.

Step forward and decide ... not to glance or look straight back,
As your pathway lies ahead, and now you're right on track.
Open hearts and minds, upon the road that you have sought,
To find true self and love, that can't be sold or bought.

Know all 'light' is so beautiful, no need to wish it true,
It's for each and everyone, not just the one or two.
'An Enlightened Experience' lies next, of what we wish to tell,
Bringing joy and hope and light ... and to fill your newfound well.

ENTER

So now the door is open, please guide them all within,
Show them your true light, and the truth it does not sin.
One glimpse of such beauty way deep inside,
They will not run or ever want to hide.

Now witness the waves of them all crossing over,
This love and light is no 'Supernova'.
But earth, moon, the stars, and the Sun,
Changed each day so you're saved by the 'one'.

Just follow your heart, the truth and light,
In shining for others, you will be all right.
So, moving away to start afresh,
The new web of life, not a complicated 'mesh'.

It will exist on love and love alone ...
No hate or anger to penetrate this new 'home'.
Encased in light for every 'being' to perceive,
To live and learn you are already free.

THE SPARK

The spark has been set and the paper alight,
It is down to mankind to live or fight.
But how long now, has the world got to go?
Has a countdown begun ... to comprehend and to sow?

LOVE AND LIGHT FROM THE GREAT SPIRIT ABOVE!

While the Earth is dark and the world is grey,
This will be brighter and returned one day.
Go and learn to follow the way,
So that both light and love; you shall seek to save.

Yes, peace and goodwill to all of you;
Please open your hearts and minds.
Not of what is yours or mine,
But that which leads you to the divine.
Now go and take care not to throw away,
Another chance ... to live, we pray.

FLOW

Water flows like love down a stream,
Rolling pebbles and stones to their origin it seems.
One by one they all seek a true home,
A shore they will need, no more worry to roam.

Rays from the sun they shine down upon the water,
Increasing the temperature and molecular structure.
The rays of love are doing just the same,
So listen to the heart and do not focus on names.

Begin the journey and move slowly at first,
Gathering pace now anew and then quenching your thirst.
Drink in rays of the light to strengthen yourselves,
Gaining speed and new knowledge by embracing each 'self'.

Those seas of emotions they glide side to side,
Moving love ever nearer, upon the new tide.
Then the faster you travel feel the strength within you,
No need to cry out or to scream or feel blue.

All colors of the spectrum they are linking as one,
In brilliant wonder from the glory and the sun.
Now truth and love it all comes from the source,
And the wisdom is in knowing that we are all one.

The journey not slow, is now nearing the shore,
Arriving in time but not a second before.
A time slot for all because the pebble is you,
Radiance of your heart, with a soft gentle hue.

So home safe and sound and a new life begun,
A wondrous thing indeed ... when your reborn my 'son'.

Rhyme & Reason

Such a welcome for all that you've never known,
In realization too that you'll not have to go.

Peace and tranquility and in love that I say,
For completing the journey and of many short stays.
If you have done the work and a job well done,
Feel the love forever … from the true golden one.

A mass of energy, one cannot comprehend,
Only the giving of love, and that never ends.
'He' seeks, and he finds ... to nurture everything,
The seeds of the stars, beyond heaven that he brings.

The circle of life goes on eternally,
You can willingly join us ... say 'yes' certainly.
Those that follow the truth, seek as hard as you might,
May those of the light, try to save and not fight.

In living things there is love ... and this is the same within all,
Because the 'I am' is in ants ... and the trees that do fall.
But to kill them with pain ... only denies you the truth,
Leaving Karmic shadows upon ground ... lies your internal proof.

INTENSITY

So much feeling of love all around,
Keeping me safe and oh so sound.
A healing inside is working away,
Each and every night and day.

Love, light, peace and tranquility,
What will your gift and ability be?
It really doesn't matter, for whatever you do,
Just live from the heart, and be kind and be true.

So, please do not cry and leave tears in the sand,
As we are right here, and we will lend you a hand.
Of golden light ... and rays that do mend,
To a broken heart ... a well of love that we will send.

The journey may begin, on a cold dusty lane,
Another old Pathway, not to follow in vain.
Remember the truth ... in whatever you do,
Forever we are one and remain part of you.

This is no trial or hard written test ...
As all is in trying, to live a life full of zest.
But many will attempt, to always be best ...
Cos' the ego will lie, and it will never give rest.

For your being and your heart,
And the self—realization goal.
Is just to find my love within...
That is Heaven sent to you all.

TREE OF LIFE

Life, light, and truth indeed,
Be one, be free and exist with no greed.
Now give not take to make progress,
And inside your hearts please love address.

Choices to make and chances to be made,
Just be true to yourself and do not be afraid.
For I am you and you are me,
So return with love unto the tree.

EMOTIONS

What is in a tear?
Is it happiness, sadness, laughter, or despair,
does anyone mind or even care?
All your emotions that are deep within,
are to be nurtured along through thick and thin.
One day at a time is all to take,
no need to stay up or lie awake.
Look to the light and love you will see,
but cry when you must as it's a release.
In truth 'Heaven' sent these emotions that 'flow',
enabling your heart to grow and grow.

CURRENCY

Within and above the strength is yours, it is always deep inside,
Forever flowing and ebbing just like an ocean's tide.
The currents of 'time' they only exist in your world,
So open your heart to listen and you will find the true 'gold'.
It cannot be made, manufactured, or spent,
It is all, it is everything, and it is Heaven sent.

COMPASSION

You are love and love is you,
Know the truth, as truth knows you.
Friends in compassion, brings compassionate friends,
So change today and set a trend.

Whether thick, thin, fat or small,
Head not in clouds, hearts free, not bound.
Glory to me, my glory to you,
We are one forever, so live in truth.

Amen.

THE GAME

What would you do in a sea so blue?
What would you do if you cried and died?
Where the sun and the horizon meet,
Do the reds and blues compete?

A shining light on a silver surface, glistening in your mind,
Now trace back the steps to find one of a kind.
Is it a name that comes to the surface?
But if in doubt, do you shout?

If a tear falls, do you feel big or small?
If life's a real 'bitch', is it time for worship?
Here in a 'symbol' you will know our name,
Hoped you like our little game.

Rhyme & Reason

WHAT IS LOVE?

Is it tangible? Is it right? Is it wrong? What is love?
More questions than answers when it comes from above.
The mind tricks the heart leaving a gap in its place,
Cast aside the false fears and these traits of our race.

When you cry, the tears flow from your heart and your eyes,
Many times have you asked me, "Oh please God and why?"
For this pain and the feeling of such hurt deep inside,
How can you do this, have you gone now to hide?

I know you could have saved them in truth, my best friends ...
So why didn't you Father, was it all a pretense?
For when they left me this morning without touching my hand,
The memory stays with me, not fading in sand.

And why did you not explain,
The need to take care,
As I never told them I loved them,
Or ran fingers through their hair.

Now they are gone, and I cannot turn the clock back,
Dear God could you not keep them, on the right side of the track?
If you could have helped them, then why did you not?
Alone now am I, in my chair do I rot?

Father, dear Father I just do not understand ...
Why their love can be taken, oh so cruelly from me,
As I sit and I stare looking out to blue sea,
Feeling so empty inside ... show me how to believe.

For these images are my ghosts as my soul now reflects,
My stomach in knots ... in my mind one more test?

Rhyme & Reason

Simply struggling to breathe with the ache deep inside,
The tears flood my heart, and I feel I could die.

The pain and anguish of them floating away,
Nothing but memories now ... in me they will stay.
Now baring my all, please listen to me,
For my hearts on my sleeve, and I would give it to thee.

I would sacrifice the 'all' that you have given to me,
Just to tell them I love them, I beg, and I plead,
And in these dark and lonely hours of death,
Know that my soul I would give, yes, I'd willingly send.

But suddenly in my mind, a bright light I see.
Where and what is it, as I am racing towards thee.
Such a beautiful and captivating pull of my heart;
In the brightness I see everything, in clouds and in parts.

Of life, my friends and those who passed over today,
Tasting true love for a second, is the wish I would pay.
I understand now that you care for everything I have known,
A lesson that divinity, is never lost or then thrown.
In the knowledge that my love, has not gone ... only called,
Passing into your light, set aside for us all.

Forgive me then dear Father, my God, the Great Spirit,
Sometimes I am weak, but have also grown with it.
Love is so special and such a precious feeling,
Not explained by mere words, or by anyone or 'thing'.

Your brilliance beyond shadows, and those doubts in my soul,
Through despair and false loss, you then showed my true goal.
You carried me, and you showed me, nothing compares to you,
Seeing light and love in all ... and understanding this is true.
I will—one day—touch their hand and their hair,
Full of joy and your peace, not to feel down or despair.

THE POWER OF LOVE

You are I and I am you,
And deep within … relearn this truth.
Therefore, who is the King or who is the Queen,
Only through searching and yearning, will you learn what I mean.

Now far away and yet nearer than near,
Live your own truth … by not living with fear.
For some of you doubt, upon this journey and road,
But choices and decisions, need the love of your souls.

In fact, your light is my light, and your life is mine too,
For all reside in my heart, and not only the few.
Those illusions become shattered and now cast aside,
As my peace washes over you, like an ever-flowing tide.

Indeed … cleansing and purifying is the power of my love,
While my grace lies in tears, which fall from within and above.
These delicate drops, of truth touch your lips,
Whilst your heart often aches … just for one sweet embrace.

For no division can exist, between both the 'you' and of I,
Unlike the differences and senses, like smell or of sight.
As entwined are we, fixed upon the goal,
To stay within bliss, such a cherished Soul.

Now angels of light, they sing out my name...
For in truth, we are one, and 'all' are the same.
So, hold on to those thoughts, yes purity of mind,
The truth for all life, all beings and 'mankind'.

Rhyme & Reason

For every creature of elements ... earth, water, ether and fire,
All resonate with, from and through me, and they will not tire.
And they are no different, for only the 'body' has changed,
But as stated before; inside we're one and the same.

So, inspire and aspire to behold now the truth,
Whether you are young or become old and feel long in the tooth!
Please try to be kind, to those behind dark curtains or false screens…
As those veils of despair, only disguise what I mean.

DECISIONS

There are many paths, but which one should you take?
As life is full of choices, though what is it at stake?
Left, right or straight onward you can go,
But backwards into darkness, to avoid as you now know.

The colors blue and red, are both one of the 'light',
So do not fear the dead ... of the dark and starry night.
The riddle you talk of, only rests in the mind,
As are not you and I, just one of a kind?

A glistening spark divine, resides within your heart,
It links Heaven and the earth-plane ... never to depart.
So if you cried and died, what would you feel and do,
Be lonely, cold, or sad ... forever staying blue?

Of course, the answer's no,
For you are in truth and love, and light,
Not false peace between two wars,
As your spirit now takes flight.

TRUST

Inside you lies your soul, holding love in heart and mind,
Learn to live and trust ... in yourself and all mankind.
But things they will go wrong, as they often do,
To cause a 'red' of anger and feelings oh—so 'blue'.
Just stop the boiling point, of a false return,
Now breathe and then relax, to start a Pathway home.

Trust your intuition ... and have love for one another,
Like the branches you extend, unto your sister or your brother.
For the tree of life sustains, and is always everlasting,
Whether paupers or a king, born as seeds and little saplings.

Know the man who only hates, mistrusts in everything,
Though 'he' can also learn, to share and trust within.
Both are two desires, of uncertain hidden feelings,
So relax the one true you, and try a new beginning.

With outstretched hands and heart, embrace all living things,
And trust in all the good, of what you learn and are experiencing.
In this your very lifetime, please know this time around,
Lift off from fear and darkness ... and the black upon the ground.

One's heart it must be open, to behold your true insight,
To fly high into the light ... of both the day and every night.
For mankind is one big family ... of that which you are bound,
So trust in them and 'self,' for then you'll all be found.

Push aside those negative feelings, with those shadows now aware,
Do not **mistrust** or even show, that you don't love, or you don't care.
As you all are of 'one', and in trust become then 'still',
Do this and don't struggle ... climb this slope, it's not a hill.

Rhyme & Reason

Now reach the very top, to see what you can see,
The love, the peace, the light ... and God's true harmony!
When you reside in joy, of one frequency and dimension,
You will learn and grow in waves ... an understanding of true heaven.

ENERGY AND FLOW

Energy and life, from no beginning and no end,
The understanding and the knowledge, is 'inside' to comprehend.
A flow, a constant flux, within and all around,
In each of your true 'self's, your soul and hearts are bound.

Your souls they are more priceless, than diamonds, pearls, or gold,
And God's love and light and energy, cannot be bought or sold.
ESP and travel are but two fragments of the mind,
Is it only for the few, or for all of humankind?

Everyone feels divided,
And concerned to grow and learn,
But do not venture into darkness,
For that is no way home.

Just try to touch and feel, the energy all around,
As you walk and also run, with your feet that touch the ground.
Know the wind that blows your hair, or the breeze that cools your face,
Comes from the land of love and light, to teach the human race.

Feel the power and the flow, which comes to you within,
One of heart, and mind, and soul ... and of your true being.
Such a feeling of pure bliss, that gives and sends light in,
Your heart rejoices in the peace ... a life eternal not for sin.

Be yourself and be true, to your 'self' and fellow man,
And in living and the learning, do the best that you all can.
So learn to live and trust, but don't just count on us,
Just be still to find your 'one', then the sooner you'll become.
You are important as each other, of a family not just brothers,
Connected by the cord ... from the Universal 'Mother'.

DANNY

A flower was born into this world,
That had already bloomed, and its petals had dropped.
A longing for a life, which I knew I'd left behind,
A longing for love, which I knew that I would find.

Crystal tears...
That fall from your cheeks,
I now catch and hold,
And kiss whilst you sleep.

A life in which I knew I had to go,
A story I told ... hard to bear ... hard to hold.
I sense the pain, in which I left to deal,
But yet there is not a moment, that all of you I feel.

Goodbye for now ... but not forever.
And believe me, I am close.
However far or near, on your paths of life...
Know that I am here.

I come with love, with compassion, with hope,
And grief is but a step, life unfortunately has to take.
So in your hand I will hold ...
A flower that was born into this world.

And in my bloom ... I give you all my love!

A NEW ERA

A new era of love ... that is so magical in its beauty,
Will branch out and touch you all ... from here unto eternity.
So stretch and link together, new cords of love and light,
For yourself and for mankind, and for each and every life.
It is easy to proceed, to be 'one' just still and rest,
And most importantly love all, your only one true test.

WONDER

When the snow falls to cover your home,
When the sun shines and melts it all away,
When the rain falls and wets your hair and face,
The wind will blow and dry you, and leave without a trace.

When the rainbow's cross the valley,
When the lightning cracks the tree,
When the rivers give life to land,
God offers new and helping hands.

When the light brings you a dawn ... to stir and wake your mind,
Gives the choice to feel alive ... and bring joy to you in kind.
When the night draws dark and close, and you turn to shut the door,
Think of all the 'wonders', that are here and gone before.

From the giver of all 'life', of what sustains both you and 'me',
Lies the mystery of it all, and what it could all mean.
So, turn within be true ... for love is deep inside,
Embrace your higher self, no fear or doubt to hide.

Just open up the heart, to the 'window' of your truth,
No more searching or to wonder ... or waiting time for proof.
For one day very soon, when you can then accept,
No more 'born' again ... without pain or new regrets.

REACH OUT

Enter—upon the pathway of truth, light, and love,
Energy—is overwhelming, and soft and gentle like a dove.
Light so bright, but not the rays of the sun,
Love is divine; it is for each and everyone.

A desire inside your heart, now to open and then grow,
A hand, outstretched, reach out past in what you know.
A touch, in peace, and in truth shares harmony,
For help is all around, it's not the end of your body.

Growth is your expansion, the search and one true goal,
Togetherness in joining, all living things and one bright 'soul'.
This beauty not defined, or felt or heard, just yet.
The creator 'is' as always, already finding that you have met.

AN ENLIGHTENED EXPERIENCE

The doorway is in front, so it is time to turn the key,
Release the fear of doubt, or is it just for me?
Now push the open door, just a fraction maybe more,
Look, yes peek inside, for love and the light it does not hide.

Take a single forward step and you will never look back,
Your pathway goes on and on, and you'll know you're right on track.
Open hearts and minds, on the path that you have sought,
Finding true self and my love, of that it cannot be bought.

Beautiful is our love, and that is oh so true,
It is for each and every soul, not just for one or maybe two.
'An Enlightened Experience' ahead, of this we wish to tell,
Bring you joy and hope and peace, and to fill your heart as well.

Rhyme & Reason

THE WELL

Deep within you is the flame ... that holds no fear or blame,
A light that is so beautiful, and inside it has no pain.
And know there is a well, around this in your heart,
It has many layers too, but not made of fragile parts.

It holds you where you are, so you can grow and learn,
Until the special day, when you are on your way back home.
Do not look internally, to the blackness of the oil,
Just look around instead, and beyond your mortal coil.

Cast a coin out wide, for a wish for all mankind,
Make it true and with no value, of the penny or the dime.
In each and every crystal, and the very source of light,
Is the energy to sustain ... and make things true and right.

So now be you and true, to all life forms on this world,
Or will feelings deep remain, and the story stay untold.
Deny whatever now, is holding you all back,
Dive deep into your well, don't ever then look back.

For love is there forever, for each of you and all,
No matter what shape or size, or whether tall or small.
And if you cannot talk, or if you cannot see,
You're always surrounded by ... love and God's beauty.

Now go and link your hands, to form a true friendship,
More action and less talk, to end all pain and one's hardship.
Uncover now the well, of your precious heart,
And then you will understand ... that we are 'one' and never part.

THE SHELL

The shell is now smashed open, it contains both food and drink,
    We hope it makes you wonder, and also feel and think.
      If you then consider, and decide to take a chance,
  You may win more than most, a true spellbinding trance.

So, break open outer shells, that block out what is right,
    To see what's deep inside, a body of love and light.
    In truth, we are all many, and so we are not alone,
But once you've then 'discovered', you'll find you're halfway home.

SERVICE

Love and goodwill ... they are always in thy heart,
For we are now together, and we will not depart.
For you are one of us ... as we are one of you,
Never feel lost or lonely, when you're part of the way and truth.

Oh, my blessed son, your life to know and lead...
Be one now in the light, so love can grow indeed.
Humble servants go and serve, wherever they may be...
Healing through the hands, nourish souls and hearts in need.

So, trust and live and nurture, for much love can fill the sky,
Let your hearts reach out from lands, no need to ask the why.
The creator's seeds of life, all grow in love and light,
Forever sown within ... a hearts eternal flight.

HEAVEN AND THE PLANES

You may or may not believe, if you read and want to leave,
Just accept with outstretched hands, or bury head within the sand.
As such energy and love, is within the light vibration,
A love that God bestows ... is free for every nation.

To every living thing, in existence and all time,
In galaxies and new worlds, its beauty is sublime.
The true light does not fade; it sustains both night and day,
Indeed a special place, within a Heavenly wondrous stay.

Of this and things to come, is experience for you and all,
To share and to then live, in the never—ending goal.
The creator has made this all, to be drawn towards the presence,
Such feeling of 'one' and joy, and a universal present.

RESISTANCE

We have come with open hands, of friendship, truth and light,
Writing words upon each page, which we hope will glow so bright.
Communications freely sent, that you can judge or twist or bend,
But any truth received, is from the 'one' and heaven sent.

There are so many 'beings' ... a source of help unto you all,
If you look and try to turn, within your heart you'll hear the call.
Just drop those false commands, and finally ask the question,
Find your light your glowing flame, in your own one true direction.

So, we do not come to shout ... deride, or point a finger,
All for so—called 'progress', or a tail with a right 'stinger'.
For what we have described, may disagree with what you know,
A calling from inside you ... is willing you all to grow.

We hope and pray that you, can turn from darkness and decay,
A gentle growth and flow, turn to light is the best way.
We hope that you then talk, and share this all about,
To trust in your abilities, with your gifts don't cry or shout.

The final wall and barrier ... is but you and only you,
Don't stop yourselves from being, what you are and also do.
Believe in freedom and the truth, and in democracy for all,
Feel the love for humankind, in living things and on all 'fours'.

God almighty the creator, gave birth to burning sun's,
Time for loving cords ... to unite and become 'one'.
Your new home that now awaits, is for all the love and light,
Divine sparks in every heart, forget time of day or night.

Here is a final question, would you take part or then ignore,
Making up your mind, if it's gone on to be a bore?

Rhyme & Reason

But if this has changed the way, you live and feel and think,
    We know that you will swim ... eternally, not sink.

    Our love for you remains, and it will never die,
Even though you sometimes stare, into the light and then you cry.
  Do not be confused, but seek to answer the what's and why's,
  For the light will lead you on, to lift you heart beyond the sky.

  Goodbye for now my friends, until you hear from us again,
Live in peace and light and truth ... loving words are from this pen.
    The living flame continues, yes forever and each day,
    Come on, step into light, it is your real ... **'Pathway'**.

SOMETHING NEW

To define life of the most peaceful, wondrous being,
Brings words of love … to enter every living thing.
And with contrasting opinion's that divide your soul and mind,
There's a need to pull together, to know the truth of all mankind.

You have now been shown a door; and a Pathway clear and wide,
But have you 'opened' and accepted, or did you think it was a lie?
For the energy that flows … contains its original trace,
To maintain and help you all … the entire world and human race.

So, build the bridges of emotions, as new feelings cross the globe,
Lighting up in all directions, with your heart on sleeves to show.
To reflect and rise above, as new embers of the light,
And soar high and far and wide, for deep 'within' the soul takes flight.

For today is a new start, that each of you could make,
Consider there are no boundaries, only joy and bliss at stake?
In participation and togetherness, of every living thing,
To ascend the cord of light, and make it chime and sing.

So now you have begun, with this book and page-wide open,
But is it a mere gesture, and simply just a token?
And is becoming 'one', still the continued goal,
To live in peace and harmony … to be kind unto your soul?

Now travel deep within, and hear these different words,
For this is really new, that no one else has seen or heard.
We hope it mends all hearts, which lay behind those darkened screens,
Be 'one' in love and light, and then define what can't be seen.

MOVING ON ... BE 'ONE'

Children, dear children of love and light,
Carry the flame ... but do not hold any blame.
Now come to the creator though never in vain,
As love, light, and truth, will always, always rein.

A promise and a sacrifice that we have made to date,
To never leave you early, even if it is too late.
Nor to worry you or place you all in shame,
As we are one together, for deep inside we're just the same.

Your experience could be turbulent, with your life so full of yearning,
But we hope to carry you through, the lessons and you're learning.
So, we trust you open up, and proceed take this book,
Your mind to read and digest ... your heart to see and look.
Take not it's real face value, but to find the inner test,
The truth inside you'll follow, 'till your 'one' at peace and rest.

HEAVEN'S DOOR

Push it open, push it wide,
Peep inside and never hide.
All to learn and all to grow,
You are God's children, in a heavenly glow.
So be still and calm and look for love it's a must,
Just believe in the light and in the divine … always trust.

REGRESSION

To step back 'In' and 'To' your past lives known,
Is not the communication that will ever get you home.
You need to turn 'within' and find the love and light,
That will truly be your guide, each day, and every night.

By regression (and delving), into your soul's past life experiences,
Leads to confusion and interpretation … of those many life appearances.
The past may be revealed, but will never shine anew,
For a living world that's gone, is no future to now carry you.

Rhyme & Reason

A FRIEND'S MESSAGE

Be you and be yourself in all that's said and done,
Be good, by connecting to the all-loving 'One'.
These 'times' are most difficult, and they try their best to undo,
All the hard work you and others … have been through and through.

So listen, please listen to your heart and to your soul,
Then go on to fulfil your only one true goal.
And pray and then be 'still', as much as you all can,
For the pen will always flow, receiving light from other lands.

So much to be learned, and soothing like a song,
And yes, you're right my son, we are ready to go on.
For we've all watched and seen, of what's been happening,
So never feel alone … if what's said is loud or deafening.

No … it is all 'inside, so turn within as you know how,
And we give you this new message, as it's for the here and now.
Yes, David we're your friends, and of a true star family,
Though you did not expect this, or had you almost finally?

You've waited for so long, and that was always of the 'plan',
But now it's truly over, you'll grow to fulfil this new 'time span'.
So be ready and both willing, and please set the time aside,
For we're forever always with you, and we will never, ever hide.

My son when you next sit, and feel you are alone,
Be prepared to grow and learn, and let it flow until your 'Home'.
Love and wisdom and the truth, is all around in every place,
And we promise to light the world … and put a smile upon your face,

But for now, it is goodbye … until you progress and then move
forward,

Rhyme & Reason

My son we always love you and will never lead you wayward.
We'll speak soon to lift your heart, so end finally with this 'note',
We simply love you all and wish to keep your soul and mind afloat.

TO OPEN … AND EXPLORE

The words that you speak, the tone of your voice and the touch of your hand,
Contains the energy from creation … to each and every land.
But do these thoughts now come 'within' … or only through your brain,
And if they race off track, will you feel it's all in vain?

Both your love and your anger, can be deemed one of same,
Though are they divided by ... an imaginary line or bleeding vein?
So every action and your deeds … flow from endless 'nought',
Lies the choice to live forever, separated by 'planes' you've always sought.
Yes a magical number, that exists from your hearts centre,
Both returns and forever spirals, on to the never, never.

It's so simple to understand, just brighten your 'self' right to the core,
To start to really know, the 'one' and only score.
That you are beautiful light, the source and frequency of love,
In everything and all directions … so don't believe it's just above.

ARCHANGEL MICHAEL

Archangel Michael and his sword of blue,
Keeping you safe right through and through.
The 'Light' and his all-blue lightning ray,
Both save and heal you night and day.

NO DIVISION

A flower and a tree are all born from just one seed,
And the rays of the true Sun, are born out from a deep need.
So, you bathe and are then engulfed, in peace and also love,
My power and grace, come from within and up above.

It is right and it is now, and it is by day and then by night,
So … discover and accept freely, and freely give out what is right.
No holding back, of what are the within and the without,
No laying still, a life of love, of which there is no doubt.

From roof tops or high mountains, those do seem to touch the sky,
No need to ever wonder, or cry out asking, 'Why?'
For you all have the gift, and the 'present' from my heart,
And 'one' forever is a promise … to never, ever part.

Amen.

KNOWN AND FOUND

To be attacked in any way … never will take place,
Ask, 'Why not by now?' … if it really was the case.
And would fear then make you cry, to bring tears across your face,
Knowing you're not alone, the earth and human race?

Civilizations across vast space … they know that you are here,
But they do not have the right, to travel and interfere.
So, to condemn in any way, in shape or also form,
Would never be allowed, to be split or to be torn.

The intervention of the light, and the love it then endows,
Dispels the darkness and the sin, from the one and from the crowds.
But interference from mere words, can both twist and be distorted,
Just as God's love and, light and truth, can also be transported.

If you endeavour to be kind, in thought and word and deed,
The pathway of your soul can flower from its seed.
Then be cast on 'winds' of change, for forever and all time,
To 'ascend' into the light, it is your right to be divine.

THE TUNNEL

The gentle beating of the heart will stop to soon decay,
While clenched fists try to punch 'restart' … though soon are put away.
The stillness in the air now breaks with pain and fear and grief,
And even holding of your hand is soon to be released.
'NO!' screams out the cry and shriek from way down deep inside,
With shouting out so very loud, "Oh, please God tell me why?"

The soul departs a voyage again upon the one split-second,
And in love and truth there it's found, the doorway now to Heaven.
The darkness is then broken … and shattered by light so bright,
Reflections in a mirrored glass, like beautiful rays of light.

A swirling pale white mist … descends and envelopes your 'all',
When the 'inner' realization comes, of 'love and lights' true call.
Though friends and family come … and then circle all around,
But they cannot see or hear you or know you're safe and sound.

Those souls now sparkle brightly, as you drift and light envelops,
A most powerful sensation yet, now beckons and develops.
To lift and spiral you, 'above' the plane and new dimension,
Yes, dear friend it's true, beyond all doubt a life in Heaven.

There is no solid 'mass' at those so-called pearly gates,
But with energy, truth and love and the light that is your fate.
It is there for you today, and forever an eternity,
Your love entwined together, not to fall or leave a certainty.

Now upon those precious lips, falling tears that they have cried,
Of those who are so close, do not think the last goodbye.
We ask no longer fear, and know your love that's torn apart,
Will grow now even stronger, to mend your aching, broken heart.

BEYOND

The heart of the physical, has beaten to a stop,
And the flow of blood will now … congeal into a clot,
It has paused within the veins, but is no longer in vain,
While the life force holds the truth … and is never one to blame.

You have spiralled once again, through the tunnel of bright light,
That lights up the soul's pathway, but is it day or is it night?
To know truth is not beyond, so you no longer do despair,
For your reality is the peace, within the creator's love and care.

A vision or a picture will reveal its own true self,
A mirage or an image, that you debate, 'Oh is that self?'
In truth, you will connect to the 'inside' you to know,
That beauty lies beyond the barriers, you had erected all below.

It's time to now reflect, and that you are your own judge,
Your soul yearns life eternal and may never want to budge.
And as the Ascended Masters gather, in mists of love not smoke,
The elixir of love descends, one that gives you 'life' not choke.

Then pause on where and why, and on the things that you have done,
For you then must decide, are you part of the universal one?
Only inside and deep within, is the reality of your core,
To understand what you are, and of what you've been before?

The choices you will make … as you discover then the truth,
Now consider all your actions or what you seek inside the proof.
You'll find it's all mapped out, been decided by soul and 'Source',
Embark on different journeys or stay upon this course.

Rhyme & Reason

In love and light and truth, are the decisions you will take,
They are yours of ones 'free will', and yours alone to make.
To return one day perhaps, to help others live and learn,
Or remain in light forever, not to cry or shout or yearn.

Only you will know, of what has to be done,
An acceptance thus so far, and the joining of the 'ONE'.
And why a tunnel stays wide open, in both directions you will see,
Recognition of the choice … in love and light to 'be'.

EXPLORE

With a difference of opinion and in confusion different 'stories',
Leads the mind and heart astray, to the ugliness and the gory.
By changing and also thinking, 'Oh, that's a wonderful theory',
Will give you all the chance, to acknowledge the eternal glory.

Open up and understand … and to offer outstretched hands,
To grow and know together, for love and light to then expand.
And brighter they will become, on this new level of vibration,
Linking every heart and land, the whole world and all its nations.

Then you'll really see, for your 'core' wants to explore,
Of the when and the way … and also the what for.
So, discover your real 'self', and the inner one true goal,
Then you will find the truth … that through your heart you save your soul.

MOMENTUM

You move both in waves … and upon levels of vibration,
In individual journeys when it should be of all nations.
But a time will soon arrive, when decisions will be made,
And it's up to you and all … prepare right now, not haste.

You are all of 'light' … 'beings' of beauty and such splendour,
Though like molecular structure, you can change just like the weather.
Some move so very quickly, and are powerful as lightning,
While other's drift like sand or fall like stones off mountains.

Your 'inner' light and life, is yours for growth and learning,
And by reading these new 'works', you can go on from all the yearning.
You can forgive and then forget, or retain the black and hate inside,
But in clouding out the light, you're only continuing to hide.

Together be in peace, and move forward now in motion,
Links to family and your friends, on the planes of association.
For there is where you'll find, the inspiration from true existence,
To uplift and direct away, the hate and pain and ignorance.

There are many who do believe and also desire to achieve,
But some want material gain, and in false 'Gods' that they do heed.
The truth is deep within, and not religions that cast the doubt,
For they confuse and bring those wars, and tears inside and out.

We can describe to you … the acceleration to take place,
To catch those drops of grief, that fall down upon your face.
You and you alone, can increase the pace and share the 'Faith',
But you need to believe it first for this to become an open and shut case.

Rhyme & Reason

When your true desire, is to 'open' and achieve,
You can then learn your one true truth, to believe and not to need.
That we are all from 'one', but in splitting up to divide,
You can wedge and close the door, to your heart and soul and eyes.

So, understand that love, yes, your love's a special 'key',
To the door of light and truth … and eternity.
When placed into the door, turn the handle do not knock,
For God's door is forever open … when your heart and souls unlocked.

Time that can't be hidden, and mistakes of recognition,
As millennium have but passed and developed all of the religions.
But the creator gave free-will, and the choices to all heed,
A task to understand … love and light are all you need.

Know a poem contains the lines, you'll understand or then you won't,
But never pass your task, and never give up hope.
Just strive to eternal goal, that's within you and above,
Opportunities to then develop, to fly high on wings of doves.

Each step that you all take, each nightfall and 'Daybreak',
Just feel and love your life, and not just for living sake.
For you can all achieve, with belief in that you can,
Open the door unto your soul, for you're more than just 'Human'.

ANGUISH

Do you listen to your heart, or the mind for what you do?
Do you cry and simply wish, that you can just be 'you'?
And of this anguish and the pain, for the love I thought I'd found,
When faced with such decisions, will I be swallowed in the ground?

Well … fate and destiny can be played, by the one and by you all,
But do you follow now or pause … when you really hear love's call?
And is it right or wrong, to feel the way you do,
When God's word simply says … you need only to be true.

So what's the truth inside, when you only want to hide,
If 'Be you' is what 'He' said and go with flow just like the tide.
Now force the issue and the pain, which lies inside your head,
Or is it in wishing you weren't born, or worse still that you were dead?

Don't confuse these inner feelings, of 'is it wrong or is it right',
For life is for love and living, not being trapped within the fight.
Just remember, true love will survive … if it is meant to be,
For no matter what will happen, eternal life-force sets you free.

So now face up to what's disguised, within the deep and hidden fear,
Wipe away from eyes and heart, those falling crystal tears.
To move on or to now stay, is the divided choice or your true goal,
To live life as one not two, have re-united souls.

SHHH…

Shhh … shhh, a tear so divine, as it falls from your face,
Whether alone or in a crowd, or far away in distant place.
Love is so pure, that no time or barriers can erase,
Or keep you from the light, that is forever and 'always'.

So, a question often asked, 'Oh why do we all cry?'
To release oneself a feeling … that often goes disguised.
Whether laughter or in pain, as well as through one's love,
A tear is now expressed, as part of you from up above.

It truly is so special, and beyond any gift that you can give,
No need to ask, "Please God" … or whether they will live.
Because as your tear does fall and you think it disappears,
You will realise you're together, so do not ever fear.

The creator is with you all, every second of your 'time',
Help nurture and understand … your heart's connection with the mind.
For your body and your soul, and every emotion included too,
Is contained within a tear, that is made of 'Him' and you.

CHOICE

You have always had a choice and the free will to move on,
And there are decisions to be made, but no push me-pull you along.
You are so unique, and are made of beautiful light,
To shine like brilliant stars, within the deepest, darkest night.

One day when 'time' is right, then you will understand,
You are born of such brilliance … from a guiding loving hand.
So now acknowledge what you are, the inner you and God's pure love,
Eternally delivered … a gift of light within and up above.

Please decide to express your 'self' … and to learn once more again,
Of that of what is with you, to be expanded and retrain.
Or you might have just forgotten, of how to just exist,
Blinded by non-reality, the material … are you clouded in the mist?

So, blow out negativity, that has bound and binds you so,
And clearly, you'll discover, that new seeds can then be sown.
These rays of light vibrations, are so rare like divine gold,
A discovery for all eternity, you never can grow old.

Yes, everything is then born, of the creator's brilliant hand,
And we are all no different, no matter what planet, nation, or land.
So, whatever is your tongue or the colour of your skin…
You can truly live-in peace, and forever without sin.

So, rejoice and lift your heart, to the everlasting sun,
And meet and walk the truth, on a journey with the 'Son'.
Many Ascended Masters, and those angels are true friends,
Will guide you where you need, for their love is without end.

But the truth and all those choices … are yours alone to make,

Rhyme & Reason

And now you learn this too, about what really is at stake.
Your live(s) are but a glimpse, a small fragment of light not time,
A chance to grow then know, of the love and truth 'divine'.

So, now this message ends, and we hope you'll go to 'Him'.
To the one eternal home and another new beginning.
For this most beautiful peace, is more than imagination,
It is for each and every soul … so now share with every nation.

ETERNITY

You can then all be, what you only can become,
Part of the eternal source, the all-loving 'one'.
Love and light be with you, always and together…
As you are all of light, and of a love that lasts forever.

REFLECTION

LOVE ALL ... ALL LOVE.
PEACE FOR ALL ... ALL FOR PEACE.
OPEN HEART ... HEART OPEN.
REACH DIVINITY ... DIVINITY REACHED.

AMEN.

RECONNECTION

Two sparks ignite the light, bringing darkness back to day.
And even when you think you're lost, the truth will pave the way.
Your growth and illumination, both start from deep within,
When individuals connect their flame ... of love and light, not sin.

A burst, a flash, the inspiration ... perhaps in words or of a song,
Sweet memories of one God, all back where we belong.
Such movement and emotions ...tears falling from your hearts,
To know we're one together, from the beginning we will not part.

Both born and twice evolved, from the creator, the divine,
The light it does not say, of what is yours or what is mine.
But it shares and also gives, free love to hearts and minds,
For you to do your best ... don't pretend your soul is blind.

So hence this new addition, to illuminate once again,
Truth is from the 'source' ... through words written by this pen.
To be seen or maybe heard, by one or by the many,
For reflections of your soul, are not communications from the telly.

Please come and then fulfil, your individual and group goal,
To ascend the eternal hill, the true plane of all joined souls.
So now be still and ready, for eyes not opened can be deceived,
But with your heart both pure and open, you'll succeed your own true needs.

Rhyme & Reason

LIGHT AND SIGHT TO NEW LEVELS

The musical notes that flow, above you and below,
Move like many souls, but which way do they go?
Will they sing and chime, into peace of the divine,
Or do they drift into the mist, perhaps forever and all time?

With a search it now begins, even though the door was open,
To lead you now all 'in', to bestow and not be broken.
A reward for those who have, revealed the truth unto themselves,
That life is love and knowing, the 'I' and then the self.

Because inside of you is light, and you're so welcome please don't hide,
Eternal lives are there for all, climb aboard upon this ride.
So … gain ascension and a level, of love and joy, no pain,
A sacrifice and your task, but is it cruel and all in vain?

In truth no need to worry, for you are overseen,
To pastures rich and new, or before where you have been.
There is something true, in every voice or smile and thing,
Revealed through love and light, pure hearts now out of sin.

And so, the choice is truth, and yours alone to make,
And in the peace you ask, 'What is it at stake?'
But only you can then, define your goal and path that's set,
Though for me you were not born, as we've already met.

And from the burning Sun, you're everlasting in my love,
So do not ask where from, or now below or up above.
For you it's only just, and just it only is,
Therefore, do not ever worry; a soul's choice is one for bliss.

Rhyme & Reason

Now those rays fall from within, and also then without,
Please do not ever cry … or plead or cast a doubt.
For the goodness you each do, will see you shine and all come through,
As love contains it 'all', and that includes both me and you.

Then you'll see the 'Son', and ask the why, the how and when,
Open hands so now just write, with love and I both through this pen.
You freewill to go and share, to give all from your true heart,
Tell all who want to listen, that we are 'one' and do not part.

Yes 'one' and both in time, and for each and all dimension,
Revealed then is my love, it is for you and not just Heaven.
The peace, the love and light, that is forever there contained,
Is free and you are all, from despair or hate and pain.

So now, it is your moment, to truly see the light,
Within and also out, each day and every night.
Just go and make a wish, for all that's said and true,
For in my light please know I love you, so don't feel down or sad or blue.
Amen.

YOUR SECRET TREASURE

Know me, like I know you,
Want me, like I want you,
Trust me, like I trust you,
Understand me, like I understand you,
Believe in me, like I believe in you.

Then truly discover me, your secret treasure,
Keeping me close, for we are 'one'.
Remember me always, in all things said and done,
No separation, no division, and just become.
Amen.

A CHRISTMAS CAROL

Two hearts that beat as one,
Louder and louder, they do become.
Linked in truth and by hand in hand,
Travelling through time to a promised land.

Your souls drift by in search of the Son,
To pass through love of the enlightened 'one'.
And with knowledge and wisdom given freely to all,
Open hearts and arms wide when you hear the call.

As time waits for no man, beast, or being,
I am the truth, all perceiving and all seeing.
All you have to do, is to realize we are one,
Your immortality and bliss, in truth you have won.

For your goal has been set and it's the path you now take,
One's past lives and history are not now at stake.
It is the present you are given, unlike under the tree,
To find victory, not defeat, and be forever in me.

Our love and our light, which encompasses all things,
Is not manufactured by hands or can be made by machines.
For the ingredients of your body, and of the 'physical' world,
Are always erased, like I said and have told.

Please then go forth, with a spring in your step,
Try to renew your own faith, no matter what you 'get'.
And as long as you hold on, with true love in your heart,
Eternal life my true gift, and never to part.

Peace, love, and blessings to you all,
Amen.

STAR OF WONDER

Welcome once more to one and all, but deep inside heart, can you really hear my call? For I am here, there, and am everywhere ... even beside you in the next chair ... and always within and never without, so why do you wish to scream and shout?

Do not believe in false riddles or jokes, during the time for high spirits, so be careful not to choke. And as Christmas arrives, into your home and your heart, why do many souls cry and now fall apart.

With so much stress and cause for '*dis*-ease', as one-half stands and other's bend knees. Though forgiveness and joy do the many now wish, others look blank, as they cross off their list. They ask shall I give, or will I receive, when the truth reveals ... 'you all get what you need'.

The hungry and the poor, simply cry out in vain, as those who walk by, sometimes glance in distain. So, who is the happier as both expressions had met ... the rich in the wallet or within heart instead?

Do you 'shine' as the 'hustle' and the 'bustle' pick up pace, with cards to write, and oh so many calls to now make. Can you radiate and glisten as the 25th draws near, or does the eve and the day, bring out dread and new fears?

For you all have a decision, to glow like the 'Son', each day and by night, until victory is won. So please try wearing smiles, with new selfless frowns, or do you take party 'frocks', and trade them all in for nightgowns?

However, to hide 'light' away so that no one can see, just disguises the real you, and of course the real me. For a wardrobe so deep, displays the true choice, as garments masquerade, like a change in your voice. Indeed, you can even dress up, in whatever one likes, but the truth of it all, the world grips like a vice.

Therefore, who holds you in place; for it must only be self, contained in four walls, not by goblins or elves. So, I urge you to walk, and find new chinks of light, the way out and way in, as its love at first sight.

For you can discover, a new freedom and expression, as open hands lay before ... you will realize the score. The eternal goal you must reach, in unison and as one, for all can move on, to live and become.

With the pathway I set, countless eons ago, laid out before you, as your Soul and heart now know. With many people and new friends, to come into your life, some will stay single, or take husbands or wives.

All are entwined as fragments of me, and everyone is linked, and must return to the tree. Like branches and twigs, you reach out near and far, as relatives and kin, travel through time not by car.

Throughout Creation and the Universe, love reigns supreme ... opened hearts and minds know, just what I mean. Please trust within me, to search and discover, what lies in the distance, but not undercover. ·

With galaxies and constellations, too numerous to mention, simply expand your horizon ... isn't that your intention? For the Stars and the planets, they all mesmerise, but the truth is inside, and not seen with your eyes.

It is beautiful and magnificent; no earthly words could describe ... glittering prize to behold, and only beyond mind. For thoughts often trick you, into thinking what is best, forget false desire, as love does the rest.

So, while looking at the sky, upon dark starry nights, what do you wish for, go to ground or take flight? Is your head in the clouds, as some state you are, or is your heart far above, so-called madness of crowd?

One should be who you are, and what you were born unto be ... an expression of love, made of you and of me. Do not pass into shade, of past duties or time, rather walk to the glory, of the light so divine.

For every moment or step, which you take towards me; the closer I become, for I shall take three. Sincerely I wish, for your good conduct in life ... no ultimatum or test but living in love is the best.

My grace is all abundant, and is 'forever' so please trust, and having faith within me, and inside you are a must. Now rise above those times, when you cry or then breakdown, for I will protect you always, with light sent from my crown.

And even with my 'glory', there are some who do not feel, or if you turn away, from friends and family who are real. By linking arms and your hands, with neighbours as one, the world can still change, and it has already begun. This is hard to be seen, and for you to realise, when violence and hatred seems forever to rise. So, do not succumb to what the media or politics portray, but do all that you can, to help lead man from decay.

With everyday choices and these are your own; try leading by example, and not by false throne. Act then in truth, to achieve the extra mile, for always I am with you ... whether meek or the mild.

No matter if an adult, even teenager or child, what is your dream, and what makes you smile? And if I made your one wish come true, what would you ask me, and is it for you?

More money, a job, new clothes, or new life, perhaps a change of your body, but not by a knife? Do not become down, by any trouble and strife, or think you are unloved, because that is not right.

Because you are everything and in truth come from me, not separate, or divided, for that could not be. Indeed, your essence and your beauty cannot be called into question, no matter what debate or arguments are mentioned.

For you and I both know, this all to be true, simply put we are 'one,' so do not feel shame or be blue. This Christmas time then, please forgive and forget ... the pain or the anguish, by which karma may set.

Instead, please be joyful and reach out from your heart, as true love is eternal, and there from the start. As in the past and now present, time to decorate your home, live to the full and in peace, beyond speech or the phone. For the Star of Wonder, you now place upon the tree, represents a 'life' beyond dreams, and is your true 'reality'.

Amen.

KEEP ON TRACK … WITH SAI BABA

**Time to then experience, a journey straight and true,
Stuck unto the tracks, with my love it's just like glue.
No safety belts or fear, when I hold you oh so dear,
Those tickets not required, being burdened by your tears.**

So much pain and anguish, but now you're free at last,
Peace and bliss, our memories … but they come and go so fast.
I had looked at all your life, what you said, and you had done,
In truth your love eternal, has more than just begun.

**Remember my words reflect, upon the future and the past,
As you pass beside the body, some stand and stare aghast.
In visions and in dreams, I will remind you of the truth,
My body was a vessel, to be used for living proof.**

I love you my dear Swami, so please remember that is all,
And yes, received your message, of your darshan, my one true call.
To continue and to strive, to live through and in the heart,
For we remain as one, forever from the 'start'.

**So mourn if you now must, but only for a while,
As the stone was rolled away, for eternally wide smiles.
My cloth it was pure white … often orange, and next time green,
Deep within your heart, you will know exactly what I mean.**

Yes, your life it was a message and you tried to say it all,
To come unto your bosom, we waited for your call.
Both the rich and so did poor, came from Nations far and wide,
For your omnipotence and omnipresence, as none of us could hide.

Rhyme & Reason

You may think you're far away, but you're always near and dear,
It is time to stop the crying, and the shedding of those tears.
For I am always there, as you sit and when you weep,
My hands they hold your heart, and you are safe within my keep.

Okay I will go, to live in truth part of your play,
Yes, be kind tomorrow, and for you **SAI** every day.
A need of who I am, and what was born to be,
Still walking amongst us all, beyond eternity.

Amen/Om Sai Ram.

Remember!! Remember the day ... Sung by Ajnish Rai.

A SOUL'S GOAL

You strive to be 'one', yet you are already free,
And your soul is a branch or a leaf on the tree.
To then float upon the breeze and be taken by free-will,
Though sometimes you will struggle to climb up life's hill.

You journey alone, and yet we are never apart,
While a connection is in truth if the heart is ajar.
And like a door so strong, made of fine spiritual oak,
Enter in and be bathed, by my joy; lie and soak.

Emerge and sustain in your new zest for life,
Be gentle and kind; love your friend, husband, or your wife.
So, walk the good walk and talk the good talk,
And be true to your soul to fulfil your true 'goal'.

Amen.

TRUTH

Right or wrong are words in a song,
For truth is the way, from youth to old age.
So do what you feel and feel what you do,
As tears that fall, are from 'one' not two.

ENLIGHTENMENT

Short and fat or tall and lean,
Come to me and truly 'be'.
And if your black, white, yellow, or red,
How many live, or are hearts all dead?

Accept new horizons as they change,
For even the Sun seems to shine then fade.
So … why so serious, when you feel down,
Shedding those tears, to frown like clowns.

While this text reverts to Rhyme & Reason,
Humans and souls flow nation to nation.
All individuals or are they really,
When global communications, link your satellites and telly's.

In contrast, turn within, to learn and look,
As others read lines from numerous books.
Each one desires, the answers to their life,
No matter a son, a daughter … husband or a wife.

Information and guidance sought in a digital age,
But few find the wisdom, from a Sage.
And throughout all time, ascended masters came and went,
All born divine, some were burnt at the stake.

So, whom can you trust, to find the answers that you seek?
Do they lie with a guru, or in the mellow and the meek?
Just open your heart, then be still, brings peace and quiet … from the zoo,
Knowing the 'I am I' lies within … for it's the 'me' that's in you.

No need to feel downhearted, it's just a mysterious link,

Rhyme & Reason

Always gentle and loving, and way more than you think.
For I will not shout, remonstrate, or scream,
As love is the way, and I will show you what I mean.
While unveiling this truth, is a test and a task,
"The first steps unto bliss?" as you might well ask.
As illumination and divinity, go hand in hand,
In unity we fall, and united we stand.

So, it's all for one, and one in truth and for all,
As loudspeaker and hailers, now bellow out the call.
Because words upon a page, are the voice, sense, and reason,
Be it day or by night, of each and every season.

In spring, summer, autumn, or the cold,
I am the way, the door, and the true spiritual gold.
With nuggets to inspire, to teach, and to guide,
I shall reveal what you seek, as those answers are inside.

So, open up this book, to read or take a look,
For in my heart, I do hope, you'll find truth to become hooked.
As the light does indeed, expand with a new pace,
With its brightness glowing too, as all hearts fall into place.

Illumination so wonderful and beautiful and bright,
Lasts forever while awake, and in one's sleep, day, or night.
Your dreams flash and burn, deep upon and in your mind,
As they reveal in many ways, we are all one of kind.

Therefore, run, walk, or even try to crawl,
Upon the stage of love and life, no matter tall or you're small.
As character and your 'essence', can play little or big parts,
Each day and every night are only choices from the heart.

What you then reveal, is just a reflection of yourself,
But do you admire or condemn, by staying stuck upon the shelf?
For you can grow and learn, from the reincarnation act,
And a true performance in this life … puts you right back on track.

Rhyme & Reason

Know the light shines on the truth, and not upon the lies,
Take a bow and the applause, and then my glittering prize.
As this is not a trick, or any man-made gift,
But enlightenment bestowed, to reward your own true grit.

Yes, time and time again, you may have fallen down,
And tears they've often dropped, as you rightly wear my gown.
Enter now my kingdom, and be escorted into peace,
A winged chariot sent to carry you, draped in Golden Fleece.

You sit beside me now, within my heart and not a throne,
Removing ring of thorns and replaced with a true crown.
For I empower every soul ... as we are one and one is all,
Ascended Masters like my 'Son' … having woken to my call.

You see you are my love, and my light it has now grown,
So fly back unto me, and return to your true home.
Do not fritter or belittle, what is rightfully your due,
Just hold your head up high, in whatever you try to do.

The light that you all are, know it cannot tell a lie,
Simply grow 'within' to the truth, and then you will not cry.
And even if bad things happen, to those who do good,
It's beyond your reasoning, though you doubt that it should.

So do not fret or worry, of what is yours or what is mine,
For all that is now needed, is a universal sign.
"But what is it?" some then ask, and also as they pray,
"Is it magic; in these notes, the divine to save the day?"

Well ... no wand or any crystal, or even minerals or fool's gold,
Can ever shine the 'light', and of the glory that is told.
And whether you now believe, or if you think all this is fake,
I'll still love you even though, another re-birth is at stake.

Do not dwell upon the negative, but carry on as you please,
And walk the line ahead, for 'you' I will not tease.

Rhyme & Reason

Forget emotional blackmail, as 'free-will' I do send,
From darkness, hear a voice, with words of light through this pen.

I wish for you all always, for great things to then achieve,
But am sad when one gives in, to desire or to sleaze.
What you crave and think you need, are but tricks upon your mind,
Times like that you must be 'still' ... and then you will be fine.

Now overcoming doubt, and with-it false despair,
Reveals and shows each other, that you feel as well as care.
Though if you do succumb, and fall flat upon your back,
Know that I am there, no time to rest or have a nap.

Realise, those lines of energy and vibration, are very near and clear,
For I exist in everything, so far and also near.
So go forward in real motion; but will destiny then but wait,
When hearts of love and light, cast out your doubt, the fear and hate.
.
With books of text and pictures, from now to bygone age,
Each tells you a true story, in their lines upon each page.
Some just give a whisper, or even a small peek,
But truth is the Indweller, of your heart that you all seek.

So, I think you will agree, during gloom or darkened times,
A fragment of some hope, can come in glint of just an eye (I).
A sparkle and a beacon, perpetual joy is not a sin,
Your eternal goal connects, and not only from 'within'.

I ask you then and now, with all of that I am,
To try to now 'return', a wish home in this lifespan.
But these choices are forever, and always will be yours,
Though your life can be a bus ride, aboard my magical tour.

While destination is unknown, for so many that is true,
But never doubt in what you are, and in what you also do.
For you are truly everything, and so everything is you,

Rhyme & Reason

Go fulfil your one true goal; knowing your dreams they can come true.

Right now, it's time to rest, for the hand upon this pen,
As words circulate upon the ether, beloved I have sent.
So be at peace and may the light, shine within and on you too,
Enlightened hearts we're stuck together, by eternal love ... not simply glue.

Amen.

CONNECTIONS

You are all connected, by strands of Light and Love,
While a Soul is never 'born', from within or up above.
So you yearn and try to search, from both heart and then your mind,
But I reveal you're so much more ... not alone or one of kind.

Like the spider's web vibrating, upon and in the wind,
Fragments of life are 'captured', so do you think that you have sinned?
Yes nourishment for one, and maybe fear and pain another,
While the experience is for all, of this you now discover.

In the centre it connects, as each link then forms a line,
A web of life to live ... in truth and you'll be fine.
Because energy is forever and this cannot be changed,
Only those who do not learn ... will think it all in vain.

Think of it right now, upon a cold and frosty morn,
It glistens and it glows, as the Sun begins to warm.
Frozen elements they do cling, from the deep and dead of night,
Or a quiet pause of stillness, do you long to now take flight?

For peace and now this truth, will melt all those hardened thoughts,
Captured by frames of time, you had believed they could be bought.
Not by money or material, or any false and Earth-bound pleasure,
The golden centre of all life ... I reveal as your true treasure.

So know you are not trapped ... or enclosed to be passed by,
For growth and understanding, means the higher you can fly.
With knowledge now move on, and glow brightly as the 'Son',
Live eternally in peace, forever you and I as 'one'.

Rhyme & Reason

Truly, light flows from, through, and to you, so comprehend these bands of golden energy, which form rings around the earth and upon all places, are creating connections like links of a chain; entwined and embracing each other in friendship and peace and can never be broken. In fact, they are eternal, forged from and into my heart's fire, sealed with my grace and blessing to guide you towards eternal bliss ... along with a promise of this 'miracle' to have and behold, and cherish forever.

This cannot be erased, or slashed by sword or tongue,
No matter if you are black, white, or whether old or young.
So, whether a pale yellow, or perhaps a shade of red,
Truth is beyond such trickery, of a so-called fear of death.

Please know your soul and goal, for you will then prevail,
From the impermanent world find truth, so look right through the veil.
And if you are awake ... or deep within a sleep,
Seek the light which shines bright, as day and night I both keep.
For inside is where you'll find, every answer that you seek,
From me who is the 'I', and the 'I am' who you now meet.

Amen.

EVERYTHING ... I AM

What I am 'is' who I am, and who am I is what I am.
This is no riddle or joke to confuse, as I do not constrain and never abuse.
Now your life and journey and the quest of your soul,
Have tasks to complete, so fulfil then your goal.

Away from the past to live within the present,
Find your true heart and the love, which shines evanescent.
Karma and the sin ... to cast aside just like a stone,
Return unto the crown and be kept safe wrapped by my gown.

For Angels and Archangels, they watch your every step,
So, trust now in your heart, and not inside the head.
Return to be 'still' and rejoice in the love,
For the truth is within you ... not below or above.

Well, this is no mystery or complex issue to discover, manipulate or bend, for you are I and I am you. As such, know and understand...

My love is your love too, in all that I do send,
For everything I am, be it Father, Mother ... friend.
In every leaf and rock ... and on land, sea, and air,
You will find the truth and light, for I always reside there.

So place trust inside your heart whilst learning how to care,
Know your heart can still be open, to both feel and to then share.
Within your dreams and wishes and those prayers that I do hear,
Cherished laughter and a smile ... or those tears which I will clear.

Rhyme & Reason

For I recognize all hearts, filled with emotions which can scar,
Yet in truth there lies the door, for my heart has been ajar.
Though love feels often taken, and may seem to cause you pain,
But for those and this 'experience', know it's never in lost in vain.

Realise 'love' cannot fade, like your memories may well do,
For the heart retains my truth, and that truth still lives in you.
Know my light and my love … are for each and everything,
So open heart and mind and soul ... to rejoice and also sing.
Then you will understand, deep down and way inside,
That I am you and me, and never shall I hide.

Amen.

1000 ('I's)

Who is the 'I', well don't you see?
And where am I ... if I am thee?
For I am you and you are me,
Not born, and yet ... both from the tree.

Rhyme & Reason

REUNION

**Time to then experience, a journey straight and true,
You're stuck unto the tracks with my love it's just like glue.
No safety belts or fear, when I hold you oh so dear,
Tickets aren't required as you're burdened by your tears.**

So much pain and anguish, but now you are free at last,
Peace and bliss our memories but they come and go so fast.
I looked at all your life and what you said and all you've done,
In truth your love eternal, has more than just begun.

**Remember my words reflect, upon the future and the past,
As you pass beside the body, some stand and stare aghast.
In visions and in dreams I will remind you of the truth,
My body was a vessel, to be used for living proof.**

I love you; I love you so please remember that is all,
Received your message and your darshan, and for my one true call.
To continue and to strive, to live through and in the heart,
For we remain as one, forever from the start.

**So mourn if you now must, but only for a while,
For the stone was rolled away, to bring eternally wide smiles.
The cloth may be pure white or orange or maybe green,
Deep within your heart, you'll know exactly what I mean.**

Your life it was a message and you tried to say it all,
To come unto your bosom, we waited for your call.
Both rich and the poor came from Nations far and wide,
Your omnipotence and omnipresence, as none of us could hide.

Rhyme & Reason

You may think you're far away but you're always near and dear,
It's time to stop the crying, and the shedding of those tears.
For I am always there, as you sit and when you weep,
My hands they hold your heart, and you are safe within my keep.

Okay I will go, to live in truth part of your play,
Yes be kind tomorrow, and for you SAI every day.
A need of who I am …and was born to be,
Still walking amongst us all, beyond eternity.

AMEN/OM SAI RAM

I AM...

I am the shoreline and your safe harbor.
I am the firm and smooth ground you walk upon.
I am the air you breathe.
I am the Sun that warms your face.
I am the hope of your change.
I am the faith, which burns away doubt.
I am the tears that melt your heart.
I am the attainable dream of bliss.
I am the goal of liberation,
And I am your true desire.

I ACCEPT

I accept your strength and your weaknesses.
I accept your kindness and your devotion.
I accept your pathways, which each one of you take,
And I accept your Love and Light too.

RECOGNITION

When you sit in silence, I am the air that fills your lungs,
For the breath of life it beckons, let the joy be said or sung.
And when the sunshine falls, and rests upon your face,
I am forever in your heart ... and also every place.

Then should you now hear bird song ... like a gentle lullaby,
Realise I'm with you always, never to say goodbye.
And if you smell sweet fragrance, from colourful blooms and petals,
Know I am the only scent ... to perfume your heart not made of metal.

When you bear brief witness, to natural laws and phenomena,
You just gaze within the moment, of a fragment of my power.
And if you touch and wipe a tear, that falls now from your eye,
Appreciate the truth of 'self' ... that is the love of you and I.

So, allow the resonance of our peace,
To continue to shine and grow,
And overcome those false emotions,
By stopping them in their flow.

Please continue to become 'still',
And you'll partake in sweetest pill...
No Pavlov's dog or pretence,
Will be your guide or your defence.

Therefore, always follow your heart,
And in doing so you'll know mine,
For all go to love and light ...
Just remember you're divine.

Amen.

OUR TEARS

I hear the sounds so pure, just like a gentle lullaby,
And my eyes they now glaze over, as again I ask God, "Why?"
These musical notes are soothing, as if they are sent from heaven above,
But I sit and question my heart ... for deep inside a broken love.

You see we're missing 'Bubble', he's such a tender loving cat,
That you could ever wish for, to sit upon your lap.
He really is so special, that we do hope to find,
As he is part of God ... such love for humankind.

Still, we have the sadness, as we struggle to understand,
But strength soon comes within, it's God's guiding, loving hand.
'He' holds us close and tight, as he knows of what we're going through,
Then whispers to our hearts, **"Love is not divided ... or ever torn in two.**

And because you're all so precious, don't feel down or blue,
Just know that Bubble's safe ... in my love and light so true.
And the experience of hurt and pain, are part of your soul's growth,
Even though it feels right now, such words just seem a joke.

Oh, your tears they are so golden, as they drop upon your face,
And your love is both eternal, as it always leaves a trace.
Yes, cords of truth and light, across dimensions and of time,
For in beauty and in peace ... no death, for I am the divine.

So, now fill your hearts and go, with those memories that are real,
And nothing and no one, can take away what you both feel.

For the love your tears contain, will erase the heartache and the pain,
As your connection to each other, is sustained within my heart …
and stays forever in my name."

Amen.

REFLECTIONS

I sit at the water's edge and wait,
And the wind cools my face … time to contemplate.
Of life and the elements and the splendour of the sun,
Trusting in God, the universal source and all loving 'one'.

White surf now sweeps elegantly to the side,
And damselflies are mating as they glide on the tide.
A lone bird swoops and descends for a drink,
Thoughts now emerging but I must pause while I think.

Sounds fill the air, some sweet as a song,
The buzzing insect resonates, life simply rolls on.
Sunshine now glistens, a golden bridge across the sea,
Such warmth is refreshing, just as your love that's in me.

It's so peaceful and tranquil … I could stay here forever,
Knowing dear God, we'll always be together.
But while on earth-plane, there's a job and my work to be done,
To be true in life, light, and love … and to try and have fun!

DEAR FATHER

Thank you:

For hearing me and understanding me,
For knowing my needs and coming into my life.
For your love, your peace, and your beautiful light,
For being in my heart and telling me that we will never part.

I wished to open my eyes, so that I can truly see,
To look beyond my senses … which can blind the truth inside me.
Your divinity shines above and also through my soul,
To be always with you, I hope … is my only true goal.

Dear Father, you are everything, and everything is you,
So, please guide and protect me with your loving grace too.
May your mercy bring healing to all those in pain,
That this journey and discovery will never be in vain.

DISCOVERY

The stars glint and shimmer in the haze of infinite space,
Whilst the brilliant full moon casts shadows … across many a startled face.
And we search across the horizon, for we know it hides a place,
An opening and a goal, a destination for the human race.

The doubts and our fears, bring the questions deep within,
As the maddening world will teach and lead us all to sin.
But an outstretched hand now offers, and it gives and does not take,
To secure a place beyond, though we think we have to wait.

Our gain can come through pain, which will lead us on and on,
To strive and conquer ills and discover we all 'belong'.
So, be free and live in peace, the world's leaders need to heed,
To discover your true self … and to fulfil your own true need.

STARS

You will often feel that you are so very far away,
But that does not mean it's forever and a day.
Because a heart cannot fade either through time or in space,
As it resides within truth and is open to light and love always.

So, as you witness the stars which shine deep into night,
Know there's family and friends and always hope on your side.
And alone you are not … and never can be,
Even when you sit and you gaze, into my infinity.

THE PEARL

There is a pearl within the ocean of life,
This beautiful planet created, by peace and not strife.
Such a gift for us all, to learn and to love,
And swim with the flow, in golden light from above.

For the treasure we seek comes not from the dive,
Its inside your heart, and then you'll know why.
Perhaps it's a test, to safeguard everything we know,
Or maybe it's too late, to protect its heavenly glow?

So, when you gaze upon stars and also blue sea,
This splendour of creation … of both you and of me.
Just breathe deeply and rejoice, and perhaps then forgive,
Please erase darkness and decay, so we can all live.

THE STRUGGLE

From school days and school plays maybe 'life' is a stage,
Just performing and acting each job for a wage.
You turn some corners to find your set upon,
By the audience and the world all clambering to get on.

The weight and the burden of so-called problems carried around,
Unbearable now, on knees, as your face hits the ground.
Time to reflect upon the truth you'd forgotten … but now found,
That you can never give up … or let life grind you down.

TIME

Contemplation of what you've done, and also where you've been,
From the scuffing of your knees to the understanding of the 'key'.
Each year a new fragment, or a page of this your life,
Just a friend or when in love, become a husband or a wife.

The hands upon the clock, they just tick … go on and on,
Never ending … time expanding, like the words within a song.
You may look for a brief pause, and a break within the past,
But then you'll soon realize, physical life it never lasts.

You are a soul and wonderous being, of beautiful light and love,
And given gift of your free-will, from the wonder up above.
So, learn and look always, for inside you lies the truth,
Becoming one with the creator … and you live eternal youth.

IF

If wishes came true only one would do,
to be reunited with Moose.
Just one touch or a little kiss …
to let you know how much you are missed.

I think about you every day, and wish I could say,
"Hello Moose, we've missed you."
But instead, I just brush the tears away,
and think maybe … one day.

SPIRIT AND SOUL

Dear child … my living essence of the tree,
You cannot yet see but can only hear me.
You made a step forward by opening your mind,
And you'll be learning that we're all … simply one of a kind.

Your tears of love that fall and do shine,
Contain the light that is yours and is also of mine.
While certain events happen and they cannot be changed,
The karmic slate to wipe clean and must be forever erased.

You are a link and exist in more ways than one,
And your sensitivity will increase, and you will become.
So, when you think you're alone and do not understand,
Reach out with your heart and then know, I'll be holding your hand.

For time goes by and what's left can't be traced,
And you ask the why and what for, as you look for my face.
Well know that I'm safe and surrounded by love,
And my love for you and all, comes from within and above.

Religions need to be understood and boundaries pushed aside,
By touching the true love that's all around and inside.
Just look for the light and the truth in words said,
Then you can move forward … to know I am not 'dead'.

ISSY'S THANK YOU

Father Almighty...

Thank you for the shelter from the storm, and for the clothes to keep us warm.
For the birdsong and the trees, for the work done by the bees.
For the food upon the table, and for being well and able.
For our world and all the nations, and for your communications.
For your assistance when we fall, and for listening when we call.
For your son we trust in him … David, me, and Jim.
Now that this 'meeting' has come to an end,
We thank you again our father … our friend.

Amen

FURTHER READING

You will find your own guidance and inspiration every day, week, month or year as nothing in life is ever by 'chance'. Each Lesson will simply be the most appropriate for your needs at that time, helping you to find inner peace and balance, as well as your own spiritual education, growth and understanding. Here is a selection of my favourite books and authors, which I hope you will enjoy reading too.

Sai Baba Gita-
The Way to Self-Realization and Liberation in this age.
By Al Drucker
ISBN 0-9638449-0-3

Conversations with God
By Neale Donald Walsh
Book 1 - ISBN 0-340-69325-8
Book 2 - ISBN 0-340-76544-5
Book 3 - ISBN 0-340-76545-3

The Message of a Master
By John McDonald
ISBN 0-931432-95-2

The Celestine Prophecy- An Adventure
By James Redfield
ISBN 0-533-40902-6

Anastasia- The Ringing Cedar series -Book 1
By Vladimir Megre
ISBN 978-0-9801812-0-3

A Course in Miracles
By The Foundation for Inner Peace
ISBN 0-670-86975-9

The Winds of Change
By Stephanie J. King
ISBN 978-0954242169

The Day my life changed
By Carmel Reilly
ISBN 978-1-84509-420-1

Confessions of a Pilgrim
Bu Paulo Coelho
ISBN 0-7225-3293-8

A Mind of your Own
By Betty Shine
ISBN 0-00-255894-7

Angel Inspiration
By Diana Cooper
ISBN 0-340-73323-3

Chicken Soup for the Soul
By Jack Canfield and Mark Victor Hansen
ISBN 0-09185-428-8

The Complete Book of Dreams
By Edwin Raphael
ISBN 0-572-01714-6

The Bible Code
By Michael Drosnin
ISBN 0-297-82994-7

Noah Finn & the Art of Suicide
By E. Rachael Hardcastle
ISBN: 978-1999968816

Noah Finn & the Art of Conception
By E. Rachael Hardcastle
ISBN: 978-1999968861

GLOSSARY

Spiritual Guidance & Education

Abundance: Awaken your consciousness, to the knowingness of your own creative abundant energy, a part of creation.

Affirmations: Help us to purify our thoughts and restructure the dynamic of our brains. Personal affirmations are positive, specific sentences which need to be in the present tense, often repeated several times to encourage or motivate yourself. The word affirmation comes from Latin 'affimare', originally meaning "to make steady, strengthen."

Amen: A Hebrew word that means "so be it". Usually said at the end of a prayer, we are asking God, "Please let it be as we have prayed". NB. When people place their hands/palms together it signifies a negative and positive flow of energy. The left receives and the right sends. The same hand gesture is a customary Hindu and Buddhist greeting called Namaste but is also used when leave-taking too. It is sometimes spoken as Namaskar or Namaskaram.

Angel: The word "angel" is derived from the Greek word angelos which means 'messenger'. They are divine spirits, each of God's consciousness and these beings of light intercede for us, answering our prayers and calls for help.

Archangel: Hierarchs (leaders) of the Angels.

Ascension: Is the process whereby the soul, (having balanced /removed karma and fulfilled its divine plan) merges first with the universal /Christ consciousness and then with the living presence of the I AM THAT I AM. Once the Ascension has taken place, the soul becomes a permanent atom of the 'Body of God'. Please remember, your ascension is not something you plan for or takes place on a certain date. You are actively choosing a process to evolve into higher consciousness ... through expanded awareness and integrating the higher reverberation of your spiritual self. So, the act of ascending; is to climb to a greater plane/dimension which involves total transformation on all levels (all that you are) ... realigned with divine love. In Christian belief, the ascent of Jesus Christ into Heaven on the 40th day after his resurrection ... his return to sit on the right-hand side of the 'Father'.

Astral Projection: A breaking free by the astral 'body', believed to occur just before death or during some dreams. Also known as out-of-body experience (OBE).

Assumptions: You must remove all assumptions. Children are getting 'raised' and many of their parent's beliefs are being superimposed upon them. But how can anyone perceive 'God'/Creator/life-energy when they do not even understand the full nature of 'existence'? Do not assume anything ... you only need to experience it.

Atma: The soul, universal consciousness.

Aum: This is the universal, sacred, and indestructible sound. The frequency of the same word that went forth as the origin of creation ... the basis and root of all sounds of your existence. By sounding the AUM comes our oneness and can provide many benefits to the body and mind. It is a spiritual process unaffected by culture or language and is the pathway to how your energies function. Each letter stands for a component of our divinity and is intended to be sounded separately ... with repetition and great awareness as the reverberation flows within you, moving from the navel to the tip of your nose. (Remember to pronounce the letters as Aa's, Ooo's and Mmm's). The A comes forth from Alpha (our Father) as the initiator, the creator, the beginning of consciousness of being ... the thrust of power. The M is the is the OM (our Mother) the conclusion/ending... one with the Holy Spirit–therefore the positive and negative polarities of being are pronounced. From the A to the Om, all the vastness of creation is contained and so the U in the centre is the cup cradling you (the centre piece)—the real self in universal manifestation—so, A-U-M is the Trinity in unity. In the East, Hindus refer to the Trinity as Brahma, Vishnu, and Shiva ... the relevant forces of Creation, Maintenance and

Destruction. In the West... the Trinity is Father, Son, and the Holy Spirit. NB. The meaning in Sanskrit is "I bow, I agree, I accept". I bow before God Almighty, I agree that I am the 'son', and I accept my immortal destiny.

Aura: An invisible emanation or field of energy believed to radiate from a person or object.

Auric Field: Your chakra system, subtle bodies and other subtle energy points create an interconnecting field of energy around the physical body.

Awareness: Is vital to your progress as a seeker to connect with your divine nature. Therefore, you must become aware of the external chatter which detracts from your inner enquiry. Do not just 'observe' but give your full attention to your consciousness—not the body and mind. And it will help if you only focus on one activity at a time ... so do not multitask. This way, divinity will manifest through you! Remember, the less you do, the less personality is involved and the more 'aware' of life you become.

Balance: We know that karma is action, and all your experiences of joy, misery, happiness, and suffering happen within you. Once you have truly grasped the fact that this encompasses your entire system of mind, body, soul, and energy, it can be the springboard to finding true balance. This becomes easier if you don't let the mind work against you ... a necessity to experience the divinity and bring brilliance into your life. So, try to attain this through every aspect your physicality, your diet, thoughts, sleep, posture and breathing ... everything!

Bliss/blissful: This is not a goal or attainment in itself. You need to make it your purpose, the foundation and way of your life. Everything else plays out from this.

Body: The vessel (some call it a shell, overcoat, or even a bubble) which houses our senses through which we perceive everything. The physical body is also shaped by our evolutionary and genetic memory. It thrives or withers by the food we eat, inherited from Mother Earth, and nourished by creation. In addition, it allows the faith and goodwill of the divine intent.

Bondage: What we have created for ourselves materialises from nothing more than our likes and dislikes. Bondage also refers to the identification we have placed upon our bodies and minds, and not with people, places, or material/physical objects. It all lies in your mind ... your thoughts. One who considers themselves free becomes free. One who considers themselves bound remains bound. So, you are what you think and therefore if you think you are just body and mind you are ... if you think you are boundless you are! Ironically, use your thoughts to go beyond the bondage of your thoughts! Remember, there is no bondage in consciousness.

Causal body: The highest and innermost 'body' which veils the Atma/soul. A doorway to higher consciousness.

Chakras: The Chakra 'system' is a vital part of our mental, emotional, physical, and spiritual 'bodies'. There are 112 funnel-shaped energy points within... and 2 'outside' of us.

Consciousness: Intellect without memory ... pure and unsullied by the mind's impressions and body experiences.

Compassion: A frequency of divine love coming from the soul through the heart chakra.

Death: The important aspect here is that you must experience to 'know'. Therefore, one has to acknowledge what you do or do not know, and what you believe or disbelieve too. Death is fiction, death is life, death is a continuation. When the body dies it has become unsustainable for life (your soul), so the conscious mind moves on, retaining all qualities bar discrimination. We need to relate this to karma yet again, for it acts like a bubble retaining the soul within the body. Imagine the bubble has burst and the air within now merges with totality, and so becomes enlightened.

Decrees: Relate to the science of the spoken word. A step up from all prayer forms both East and West, they combine prayer, meditation, and visualisation, and place a special emphasis on affirmations using the name of God—I AM THAT I AM. An effective method in balancing karma, spiritual resolution, and soul advancement.

Destiny: People often blame a negative outcome as a result of their so-called destiny, but in doing so they place a total limitation upon their life and so cannot be free. However, it is you (and only you) who makes your life!

Devotion: All forms of devotion arise from your emotions. It provides you with a sense of freedom and comes from the heart… unlike belief, which materialises from the mind. It is what is devoid of 'you' … and allows grace to flow through you. One may experience this by allowing a greater intelligence to work through you whilst keeping your intellect at bay.

Divinity: The state or quality of being Divine.

Earth-plane: The world of material form.

East and West: East is often related to the destruction of all that is unreal… and the purification of the veil of Maya (illusion) by Lord Shiva. West is usually termed with the action of the Holy Spirit.

Ego: The ego is the unconscious/lower self and it only identifies with the body and mind. However, in truth this lower self does not really exist … it is only an absence of awareness, just like darkness which is the absence of light. So, one cannot be aware of and also ecstatic/blissful at the same time. In contrast, your reality is the infinite or higher self … pure intelligence. Remember, you do not need to 'see' to identify with the 'all knowing' … and when you remove the ego you are able to experience pure joy.

Enlightenment: Everything is lit up; you see the reality of life/existence. True insight and comprehension.

Etheric Body: This is the body charged by God with the Holy memory of all things lovely and beautiful within the substance of the divine world … in order that you may bask in that power which one day you will know to its fullest.

Experience: Only by turning inward can you discover bliss and liberation and true peace of the divine. You must experience it yourself, and this will not happen by reading a book, traveling somewhere, or when you listen to any other human being.

Food: There is a direct correlation with your dietary habits and sleep. The greater amount you consume requires more energy by the body (especially during sleep) to process it … hence the more tired you can feel. While the body needs food to survive, this has no relation to social or religious background. If you were truly starving and there was a choice of a plate of food and God's presence to appear in front of you, what would you choose to partake/digest? Your self-preservation will kick in! However, the amount you eat on a daily basis is compulsive or conscious in nature. Will you, therefore, embrace this freedom of choice or have you become a slave to this requirement? As the world endures the COVID-19 pandemic it has been scientifically proven that those who are obese have less ability to overcome the virus. The morals and ethics of how we look after our bodies (with food intake and exercise) can be encapsulated in the question … "How long do we want to live?" To help further, understand that different food can be full of positive, negative, or contain no 'pranic' (life-energy) at all … which leads to lethargy. Some foods like Honey (with hot water) are so good they break down fat, others dull your nervous system or may stop your bodies sensitivity too. The digestion of everything inside your stomach has various timescales. For example, most fruit takes about 3 hours, whereas meat could take 2-3 days! If you could imagine a piece of meat left in the hot sun for the same time it would fester and become full of bacteria. Inside you, the bodies temperature creates the same conditions, so once again the choice to have something like this (rotting flesh) inside you remains. Know too, that *protein* is that what 'protects' you, and food that is not cooked contains the largest amount of protein. Ideally, your diet should therefore contain at least 40% of fruit, vegetables, nuts etcetera. After eating, the most advantageous proportions inside your stomach would be 1/2 food, 1/4 water and 1/4 empty.

Forbearance: An important quality indeed. The spiritual seeker must appreciate that happiness in their life occurs by totally trusting in the universe and remaining in an acceptance mode. This way, one's joy and peace will always remain undisturbed and you will never feel frustrated, impatient, or let down.

Forgiveness: Is the key to connect with the open door of your own Christ-self. The quality of love is all-encompassing and all-forgiving. Learn to forgive others and most of all yourself, for true healing.

Free-will: The discretion to use or not use … the freedom of 'choice'. The question then arises over how much of your life unfolds automatically or compulsively (if it is not happening the way you want it to) rather than acting with your intelligence … consciously.

Glory: Recognise the glory of your own soul, your divine link with the glory of God, creator, universal intelligence. See and feel its glorious reflection within yourself.

Grace: Receiving God's grace can be automatic, but usually follows the effort and endeavour made by the 'seeker'. It requires non-resistance and unconditional acceptance in the reality of our oneness and boundless state.

Guru: 'Gu' means darkness, 'ru' means dispeller. Therefore, a Guru is someone who dispels darkness … to throw light on your very nature of existence.

Happiness: To be happy you must stop finding fault with anything and everything … situations, people, and things. One must surrender to the acceptance of what is because true happiness has no cause behind it. To experience this, you must know yourself by removing all dependence on external situations… which allows you to discover the true 'uncaused' happiness of your real nature—bliss.

Heart: Your heart is a gift from creation. It is the seat of your soul and the very altar of God. Comprehend that inside the heart there is a central chamber, surrounded and protected by a forcefield known as the 'cosmic interval'. This chamber is separated from Matter, and no microscope or probing can ever discover it. Only true vision—when the eyes of the body, soul and mind are in unison can one bear witness to its magnificence. Know that it is the connecting point of the powerful crystal cord of light that descends from your God presence

— which sustains the beating of your physical heart. This also gives your life purpose and a reason for integration with the cosmos. Therefore, we must cherish this contact point of 'life' by turning within to pay conscious recognition to it.

Healing: Is a letting-go process… do it every day as you hold and welcome love into your heart. Every day you have the power to express the light of your divinity to any life who needs it. Know that the healing process takes place first in the soul—spiritually and emotionally. Then the mind, mentally and visually … followed by the body, which will always reflect the state of your true and higher self.

Higher Self: A person's spiritual self, their true identity … a focus to many meditation techniques, as opposed to the physical body.

Human being: A definition which defines us. Our consciousness and intellect distinguish us from all other life forms because we know 'how to be'.

I: Most people—when saying 'I'—are referring to (or thinking of) their body or mind, however 'I' represents our 'Immortal consciousness'.

I AM: You are saying "God in me is" … so that everything you say after these words manifests in our world.

I AM THAT I AM: The name and living presence of 'God' the 'as above so below'. In the West—the path of the Mother—descends. In the East, "OM TAT SAT OM"—the path of the Spirit—ascends. The energy of your being and all that is locked in imperfection becomes a spiral of the ascension and returns to the heart of the God presence.

Identity: Your true identity is part of the cosmos. You have to shift from what the mind believes is just the physical, to that of consciousness. Without the light, your identity is like a moth drawn to and darting around the flame of truth … but charring or burning your wings to depart into the abyss of suffering and darkness … without having attained illumination and liberation.

Immortality: Those of faith and religious persuasion believe the indefinite continuation of a person's existence, even after death. Other opinions state that mental activity is nothing but cerebral activity and as such ... death brings the total end of a person's existence. In truth, immortality is the fruit of sacrifice.

Inspiration: One of the greatest gifts of your Divinity is to become the example, the inspiration whereby you move from 'unwillingness' to 'willingness'. God provides you with droplets of truth, those golden nuggets of wisdom, the fragments of creation to stimulate your thoughts and actions to 'create'. Even if you feel that you have not reached the pinnacle, or conversely feel like you have plummeted to the depths ... you retain the ability inside you to inspire.

Invocation: The act or instance of invoking, a prayer or command to a higher power, deity, spirit, God for assistance, divine guidance, forgiveness, and protection. Sometimes used in the opening of a religious festival. It is also a way of bringing the best out in you.

Journey: The most important journey you can undertake in this lifetime is from being unconscious to conscious. This includes your thoughts, words and deeds and everything within and around you!

Joy: Try to bring a feeling of lightness to your heart and a renewed joy in living. Laughter and joyous love will bring out the child in you, transmuting any feelings of negativity and heaviness within you. Make your days joyful and watch the world around change for the better! In reality, your true accomplishment is the joy you cause in the 'heart' of God ... and 'joy' derived from service reacts upon the 'body' and helps to keep you free from disease too.

Karma: Literally means 'Action' and is of your own making. Most of your actions are unconscious, played out through one's physical, mental, emotional and life-energy. Also believed to be the totality of a person's actions and conduct and memory during successive incarnations or regarded as cause and effect that may influence their destiny. Karma is also considered to be a law or principle through which such influence is believed to operate ... fate resulting from one's previous actions. However, counteracting a 'fate/destiny' scenario, it is incredibly empowering to know that each day is our own making. Misery or joy are the choice which affects the very nature of our lives. Therefore, you are responsible for your own future … it is in your own hands!

Light: The highest frequency we know. Your physical eyes can only see that which is stopped by light. However, the pure element of the 'I' bears witness to all creation because it sees without being tarnished by memory, and views everything exactly the way it is. Jesus once said, "The light of the body is eye (I). If therefore thine eye (I) be single, thy whole body shall be full of light."

Logic: Try not to get bogged down or become a slave to logic and the reasoning/propositions and conclusions of others. Validate the truth of your reality through your own experiences, for the cosmos is here and now!

Love: Love is the way you are. Love enables us to fulfil the destiny of the soul in conscious outer manifestation—a just and merciful compassion that is always rewarded by individual creative fulfilment. Through the power of love, man learns how they may impart into others the beauty and compassion that they have received from God. Love does not need to have sustenance from anyone, therefore, if you are loving … it spreads!

Mantra: A word or formula (often in Sanskrit). They attune you and govern the release or attraction of life-energy, which becomes deposited in your aura. This expands over time, gaining momentum. For example, this powerful mantra from India "OM NANORA RIJA NIYA" tunes oneself with the infinite. "O infinite God, I want your will to be done in me".

Meditation: Practiced for millennia, and originally intended to develop spiritual understanding, awareness, and direct experience of ultimate reality. Although an important spiritual practice in many religions and traditions, it can be practiced regardless of someone's religious or cultural background. It can be used with other forms of medical treatment, and as a complementary therapy for the many stress-related conditions. Types of meditation include concentration, movement, mindfulness, and transcendental. When you meditate you are just withdrawing support from your personality, you are creating a distance between your true self and your mind … in essence, observing from an elevated, clearer viewpoint. In fact, the state of meditation is wherever and whenever you place yourself in touch with God!

Mind: Eastern philosophy and wisdom state there are 16 segments to the mind. The 4 main 'parts' relate to intellect, identity, memory (evolutionary and genetic) and pure intelligence. It encapsulates our thoughts and emotions. NB. People often refer to their 'monkey' mind during meditation, but our purpose is to liberate it, not control it!

Mindfulness: Reconnecting with our bodies, and the sensations they experience. Becoming aware of our thoughts and feelings through our senses—knowing what is going on inside and around ourselves—at any given moment.

Omnipotent: Having unlimited or Universal power, authority, or force; all-powerful.

Omnipresent: The state of being everywhere at once. All-pervading, Universal, ever-present.

Omniscient: Having total knowledge, knowing everything. All-knowing, all-seeing, wise.

Path: It does not matter what route you take if you are just constantly striving for 'more'. Know that you will never reach the destination if you continually require and crave more love, more money, more success etcetera. Only the pathless path brings you the perception, the clarity and the focus needed to liberate and experience perpetual bliss.

Patience: Recognise and feel the principle of patience to release tension in the mind and body and your life. With greater awareness, an increase in your level of endurance and ability to suffer restlessness and annoyance without complaint.

Personality: This is the one and the only real difference between each human being. It reflects and manifests as our likes and dislikes in every way and form imaginable … and thus induces bondage.

Purification: A high dimensional frequency which can operate at a causal body level throughout the subtle bodies (mind, etheric, physical, and emotional), and the auric field. This transmutes lower energies and allows a new feeling of purity to filter through the conscious mind.

Responsibility: One could say this is our ability to respond to everything that occurs within and outside of us. In real terms, our ability to respond to any given situation is limitless, whereas our ability to act is limited. It is the simplest way to express our divinity too.

Self-realization: The expression used in psychology, spirituality, and Eastern religions. Can be defined as the fulfilment by oneself of the possibilities of one's character, personality, potential, and Divinity. To become 'realised' means you finally perceive what is already there! Please note … that the instruments of your perception are all outward bound, but the seat of experience is within you.

Senses: Nature has allowed you to live life through the sense organs. Eyes provide sight to beautiful scenes and all your surroundings. Ears enable sound and melody to soothe or stir your emotions. The nose permits the aroma and fragrances of creation to ignite your imagination. Taste enables you to savour nutritious food which give life and health to the body. Touch gives you the opportunity to know and feel personal contact. However, the common theme with each sense is that they all crave and desire … which only leads to your likes and dislikes creating bondage. You must, therefore, use your intelligence to control the mind and take charge of the senses for spiritual life …and make them your servants and not your masters! A true seeker will only become fulfilled this way to experience eternal bliss. NB. An old Indian metaphor captures this perfectly, "Use the intellect-charioteer to take charge of the reins of the mind and your sense-horses … if you want to reach the destination of Self-realisation".

Silence: Is that which is NOT the basis of sound. Keeping silent has an immensely powerful impact on your life … a representation of 'nothingness'. Many guides also state you should reduce what you say by 50% … and even my wife says I talk too much! Remember, silence is the speech of the spiritual seeker.

Sleep: It is well known that the body rejuvenates and even repairs itself during sleep, but whether the average human being requires 8 hours is debatable. Of course, there may be hormonal issues in play which affect the need for even more sleep too, but it is important to cut down on it. Try to arise after 5 or 6 hours, or at least as soon as you awake. This might seem difficult to action, but this may allow you to experience another 10 or more years of life! So, if by the alarm clock or by naturally waking with the dawn chorus, do not just turn over … thinking 'I love my bed', or that you cannot get up citing 'you need to recharge the batteries'. Know it is not so much physical rest you require but more the time to ease the restless mind to re-awaken the Divinity within you. Therefore, will you stand by your bed and gaze upon the imprint of your slumber? Will you continue to resist life's tasks and tests, or grasp the opportunities presenting themselves in a new day? Why not embrace your 'aliveness' to bring joy into your life and all those around you too? In reality, sleep is a death state which you enter into through instalments (inertia) whereas life is dynamic. Remember, you cannot 'enjoy' sleep, but to rest and the time for restfulness is the basis of all your activity.

Sojourn: A temporary stay; a brief period of residence.

Soul: The soul is not the object of intellect …but the very source of your intellect!

Spirituality: Going beyond the boundary of the body/senses. You experience the reality past the physical presence, and in life, react with your intelligence consciously. In essence, spiritual life is transformation!

Spiritual seeker: Many people understand that being a seeker involves making a total and absolute surrender to 'life' by accepting whatever comes their way. However, when transformation, guidance, and the materialisation of what is sought does not occur … grave doubt may arise. Then, further obstacles or suffering will usually generate the question, "Why me?" or "Why is it happening?" But this only creates a further barrier, so it is crucial not to think or ask the 'why' question! If you can only transcend the need for any clarification in all your experiences (whether deemed 'good', 'bad', or indifferent) this will finally allow the Universal consciousness and life-energy to resolve the situation for your higher good and at the earliest opportunity too.

Stillness: Being still empowers you because it allows you to be in touch with another dimension. When you are consciously 'still', the energy you access becomes a link between the non-physical and physical elements of your existence … so you are able to witness the reality of life in its entirety. In essence, you leave your perception of a limited identity behind to see and experience the truth. Understand that stillness is not sleep, which is unconscious slumber.

Time: Seconds, minutes and hours are not your true pillars of existence. It is not how little or how much time you have, but what you do with it that counts. When you are joyful, time will seem to disappear, when you are miserable … a day can feel like eternity. When you turn inward and have no sense of body, you detach yourself from the clock face and the unreal develops into reality. When you truly accept the awareness and the inevitability of the 'moment', all suffering is gone. Understand everything in creation is in this moment, whereas your mind thinks of the future (imagination) and the past (memory). So, one must be conscious and live in the moment, for it is only this moment which is inevitable!

Turning inward: When you sit still in silence, there is an opportunity to 'experience' your reality beyond the senses. In doing so, what you have previously classed as your identity (which were bound by one's sex, race, religion, and beliefs), will break free and lose its limitations.

Transformation: Nothing of the old 'you' should remain—in contrast to improvement, which is just a 'change.' As such, the object of your desires may alter your destination, but only when you stop seeking/asking/striving for what you do not have can you change the inner process of one's life. By transformation, you shift oneself to a completely new dimension of perception and experience … hence 'self-transformation'.

Tranquillity: When the subtle vibrations which surround the body become disturbed, you feel stressed. You need to combat this, so take the mind elsewhere. Visualise somewhere calm, perhaps by a still lake or a special place held dear to your heart. Allow peace to wash over you and bring tranquillity to your body, thoughts, and consciousness.

Truth: Can only be perceived and experienced, it cannot be interpreted.

Unconditional love: This form of love is not emotional and has no strings or ties. It is the only true healing power, so try to allow your heart to be activated in this way.

Unity: Is divinity.

Vibration and energy: The resonance of your true 'self'. We are all at different stages of spiritual development, so the intensity of reverberation (sound) within would indicate the energy level you have reached. Every substance has its own frequency, its own keynote. Every sound has form, and every form has sound.

Visualisation: A mental image, like one's visual perception.

Words: On this journey called 'life' it is important to live in truth, so try speaking what you feel and act what you speak.

Wisdom: 'Wise dominion' ... wisdom to nourish the mind—for illumination and the right use of the knowledge of Universal law.

Yoga: A group of physical, mental, and spiritual practices or disciplines which originated in ancient India. One of six Astika schools of Hindu philosophical traditions. In the West, it is often seen as just bending of the body, for a better posture or exercise ... but in the East, it is a contemporary science, vitally relevant to our times.

ABOUT THE AUTHOR

David has helped to conduct spiritual development and healing circles for nearly 25 years. He has also been a guest speaker—sharing his enlightened experiences to promote 'oneness'—at various Mind, Body and Spirit engagements across the UK.

Through inner-dictation, dream interpretation, meditation, mindfulness, precognition, and healing, the books he co-writes with 'Spirit' provide you with the foundation to discover your own path of truth. With a renewed sense of purpose, the spiritual guidance and education you receive can help you reach the goal of self-realization and bliss within the permanence of love and light.

David is tee-total and a vegetarian who loves the sunshine, nature, animals, and his wife!

AN INVITATION FROM DAVID KNIGHT

If you enjoyed reading Rhyme & Reason, you can download **Deliverance of Love, Light, and Truth** for free, when you join David's mission for a 'full and blissful life'.

To learn more, visit: https://www.AscensionForYou.com

Follow us on:

Facebook: facebook.com/ascensionforyou
or
Twitter: https://twitter.com/ascensionforyou

… and become part of our community who love to receive uplifting messages for the heart and soul!

Want to let others know what you think?
Please make your opinion known by leaving a 'star rating' with one-click on Amazon.com or Amazon.co.uk and/or a review at your favorite online retailer. Thank you!

www.ingramcontent.com/pod-product-compliance
Lightning Source LLC
LaVergne TN
LVHW040153080526
838202LV00042B/3147